My Armenian Heritage
By Sooren Apkarian

Sooren with Uncle Avo at the statue of Sassoontsi Davit
Yerevan, Armenia

Copyright Year: 2007
Copyright Notice: by Sooren Simon Apkarian. All rights reserved.
ISBN Number 978-0-6151-5265-3

Our father, Simon Haroutiun Apkarian was born December 10, 1887 in Shirak, Armenia. His parents were also born in the same place. My paternal Great-Great Grandfather came from Moush, and settled in Shirak. The older folks that I used to hear talking when I was a boy used to refer to my father as a "Basheeragaltsi." And I used to think that's what the name of the town was until I came to realize, as I got older and learned more about Armenian history and geography, that they put the "Ba" in front of -Sheerag, which was like saying "The one from" Sheerag. --- And the "gal-tsi" meant "gal"(coming) and the "tsi" connotes a possessive to the place "Sheerag." So that's where the word came from. Although, as I got older I realized it wasn't really Sheerag, but "Shirak." (You know how villagers have a different way of communicating, from one town to another --- and that's the way it was!) Then, when I met my paternal uncle "Avo" in Yerevan, Armenia, who came to visit me at my Aunt Ovsanna's home, he told me that
Shirak was just across the Armenian border, on Turkish- occupied Armenian lands. (I hate to hear anyone say "Turkish" or, "Russian" Armenia ---- It's Armenian occupied lands!!) He said I couldn't cross the border because it's controlled by Russian and Turkish soldiers. Avo came from Leninakan; renamed, 1991,"Koomri". Our mother, Varsenik Dourian was born on April 25, 1903, in the County of Shahoumian, in the town of Shoulaver, and the State of Verastan (which is Georgia, ((P.S. Was))-USSR). Her parents, Grandparents, and Great-Great Grandfather came from Gharabagh, (in Azerbaijan) and there are 30 families related to us, still living there!

The Traversing of our Apkarians

In 1913, Simon Apkarian came to the U.S.A., worked as a dishwasher in San Francisco. I never found out how he got there, since he couldn't speak any English. Maybe, I assume, he came there by ship (Russian)--- since the Russians owned that part of California at one time (and Alaska) and still had considerable influence. Then, in 1920 he went back to Armenia, and then Georgia where he met Varsenik, our mother, and married her and brought her to the U.S.A. (more detailed in my book, "My Armenian Heritage") I think they left from Batum, and from there to Alexandropol, and from there they went to Athens, Greece. They waited in Athens for about a month, waiting to meet John Bogosian's parents, and they sailed from there to New York, arriving at "Ellis Island" on May 2, 1921. The trip took 20 days from Athens to N.Y. My mother said she was sick every day. (She had to go to the toilet real bad, once, and since she couldn't speak any English, and my father wasn't around, she "peed" in my father's shoe. ---(Laugh)--- I guess my father was making sure the Captain didn't get lost, or some important thing of that nature.) (funny??) Then, my mother said she had never seen a black man before,(on Ellis Island) who was serving food, and when she saw him she screamed and startled the poor man. After he found out what the problem was, he jokingly kept coming toward her to offer her food, just to scare her some more. They stayed in New York , on Lexington Avenue, for two weeks, at Miran's Hotel. Miran was the Armenian hotel owner. My mother, for years, used to say Mirani- hotel-uh (which meant the hotel belonged to Miran) and I thought the name of it was Me-ran-ee!

Listed below are the FIFTEEN locations my mother lived in after entering the USA!

(My poor mother --- and here my father told her, as he held her hands: "These pretty little hands will never have to get dirty washing dirty dishes." -- Huh!!)

1) Went from N.Y. to Braddock, Pennsylvania. Stayed there for 6 months; (1921).

(2) Then moved to a farm in Worthington, Pennsylvania. Brother Ted (Torkom), born here --August 4, 1923.

(3) In 1923 we moved to New Kensington, Pennsylvania. From there we moved to Arnold, Pennsylvania, where brother, George(Goorgen) was born, October 21, 1924.

(4) Then, moved from Arnold back to New Kensington, where I Sooren "Sam" was born-- September 23, 1926. (These cities were about 5 miles apart.)

(5) Then, in 1928 we moved to Dearborn, Michigan (Ruben Mekitaroff's father's house; 2751 Akron. Stayed-there one year! (Two family flat; we lived upstairs.)

The following houses are in Dearborn.

(6) In 1929 we moved to Ralph Kasparian's father's house. North-end-of Holly St.

(7) In 1931 we moved to Wyoming Ave. (originally called Mulkey St.)
It was behind Salina School, Southwest end of playground. (Pete, John and Stavros Geftos lived upstairs.)

(8) In 1932 we moved next door to the Roumanian Church, in a small house on Holly St., near Lowrey St. (Nevart Gopigian lived there later on; whom brother Ted married in 1949.)

(9) In 1933 we moved back up near the North end of Holly Street again, to Mr. George Katchadourian's house. (10) In 1934 we moved a few houses south of there, upstairs of Jimmy Shaker's house, where sister Rosie was born. (I was running up and down the street yelling for my brothers to tell them we had a baby sister born at home.)

(11) In 1935 we moved to Salina Street, South of, and next door to the Fordson Bazaar (a small house at the back of the lot. -- neither one are there, today.)

(12) In 1936 we moved, about 100 yards north, on Salina Street, in back of a coffee-house, 3 family flat, next door to the Damian Hardware Store: Pete, John and Mary Damian children.

(13) In 1937 we moved to a 4 family flat on the corner of Bland Street, off of Miller Road, by the Rouge River. (We used to cross the railroad tracks and walk a mile to school. This was the first year we had a radio at home. I think father bought a 1934 Ford this year. Ted broke his leg riding a bicycle.) Brother John was born here.

(14) In 1939 we moved to a small house at the back of the yard, on Akron Street. John Shakarjian lived next door, North side. They bought a new Ford. Life was getting better!

(15) In 1940 mother bought a two family flat, on the corner of Akron and Welch Street. Sarkis Halibian used to live upstairs, Bobby and Virginia Kazaroff used to live downstairs. The Halibians moved out, Kazaroff's moved upstairs, and we finally moved into a place we could call "home"! Sister Deanna was born this year. Our mother used to put money away, without telling our father about it, in order to save enough money to buy a home; otherwise our father used to loan money to other Armenians and they would never pay him back (some, "friends"!) God Bless Armenian mothers!

What goes through the minds of Armenians throughout the world? Does the desire to return to their homeland still exist? What about their children-- the ones that have never, seen the 'homeland' before. Do they dream of seeing it? Do they crave to see where their parents and ancestors came from?

Being the first generation to have ever been born outside of Armenia in the Apkarian (Simon) Ancestry, I will attempt to answer the foregoing questions for you, in order to instill a burning and curious desire in your minds. To generate the magnetism I felt to return to the land of my parents and ancestors.

As one of six children, I still can't understand why I was the only one who got carried away on Armenianism. I eat, live, and sleep with the thought-of regaining that parcel of land that justly belongs to all the orphaned Armenians, who suffered from death and persecutions by the Turks. One may question why I should feel so strongly for Armenia, being an American-born Armenian. Can I love my father, any less than my mother? Although I was borne by my mother, the blood in me is my father's. And, being a Christian, and employing my personal theology, I feel that we would be denying God's existence if we failed in recognizing our ancestry.

Since my childhood, I spoke Armenian before I could speak English. Most of the conversation and thinking at home was Armenian oriented. The community I lived in was interspersed with Armenians; and social affairs my parents attended were Armenian. How else was I supposed to think, if not Armenian? Looking back at it all; I can only thank God for creating all the conditions that formulated my Armenian ethnical, ethics. Had we been more affluent, the social conditions may have been different, and, I may not have had the good fortune of associating with as many Armenians. not having the good fortune of others who, had relatives in this country, I always wondered what it would be like to have aunts, uncles, and cousins. For 44 years, these thoughts haunted me, and in 1971 I had the good fortune of an extended vacation (13 weeks company-paid for United Steelworkers Union of America) and decided this was the year to go to Armenia (Hyastan.) Neither my wife nor my mother could make the trip with me, for numerous reasons) so I went alone. I even asked my mother-in-law 'Verkin' to accompany me (and she was undoubtedly one of the world's most nervous women) who had been orphaned through the Turkish genocide as I felt it would be the last time she'd ever see Armenia again and even she refused!

For years, I had been corresponding with my mother's only living brother, Marklen (who was six months younger than I) and one of her three living sisters, Ovsanna, in the past year. I wrote them about what day I would arrive in Yerevan. They were anxious to see me, or any of our family for that matter. I got my papers in order and the U.S. State Department sent me a letter informing me of the DO's and DON'T's of the USSR, and I presume anyone who hasn't visited would have become equally suspicious and apprehensive.

September 6, 1971

When I was leaving the Detroit Metropolitan airport all my loved ones and friends were there to see me off. It was really some experience. I felt quite like an Ambassador going on a special trip. I didn't know whether to laugh or cry. How could so many people care for me? You'd think I wasn't coming back!

When I got to New York to change planes on the connecting flight, with the large group of Armenians from California, we found out that we were travelling to London, first, and then on to Moscow, and on a Russian jet at that! And this was supposed to be a 'direct' flight! I noticed some Armenians occupied at some electronic machines and I asked them what they were doing, thinking it was another prerequisite of Russian protocol that we had to incur. Then they informed me that they were filling out flight life-insurance, in case the plane crashed. Never had that occurred to me. The first and only plane ride I ever had was on a 25-passenger company plane and I hadn't thought about a plane crash on that, let alone on a large jumbo jet. I thought how stupid I was, for not having considered my family's welfare and duly filled out a policy and mailed it home. (Was I supposed to feel better now, if I got killed?!).

The plane trip was wonderful, although not as roomy as our American jet. The stewardesses were very efficient and business-like, but they must have been trained not to smile, in order to give us Americans the impression that everything was under control, by a government that meant business ! The flight lasted about 7.5 hours and the trip about 11 hours in total.

We stayed in London about an hour and 15 minutes for refueling, and they let us walk around there, to shop in the airport. London is the most crowded airport I've ever seen. People from different countries were waiting there like a herd of cattle; poor accommodations and restaurant. You can purchase linens and jewelry, liquor and tobacco at good discounts, there.

There was a 6-hour time difference from Detroit to London. On - the same day, September 6th, we arrived in Moscow, 7:30 P.M. Moscow time. We went through the passport line, and from there, to go get our luggage. We went nuts looking for all the luggage of the people on our tour. --- A couple of women "lost" their bags! (From the more experienced "Soviet" travelers, you quickly learn that those "lost" luggages are deliberate -- it's another method of reassuring that dissidents of the Soviet policy don't come back!)

We had to wait one hour before we finally got to the Customs Inspection they kept giving us the runaround --- from one spot to another -- telling us to take our luggage from here to there and regroup, and you'll be inspected! --- After the "fourth" time, I was getting tired of moving luggage for some of the older women! Any idiot could see that the whole procedure was deliberate, because we were "Americans" -- from the United States! There were other groups from recognizable countries -- and they were just walking right through, with personal Russian escorts! --- (Don't forget --

this was in the middle of the "cold-war" era.) But what irked me, more than the Russian irritation, were the three younger guys in our group, who had cameras strung around their necks, who didn't raise a finger to help their "mothers"! (I wondered.- "Where in the hell were these guys brought up?!") ------ Finally, we went in for "inspection!" -- And guess who was "first?!" Me (at 45) and an, older man from California. As they brought us into the room, they gave us a list and told us to check off, or write everything of value that we were bringing into the country: Currency, watches, gold and diamond rings, etc. As they went through my wallet, checking for money verification, I heard the Customs official ask this older man why he hadn't claimed the $50.00 that they pulled out of his Suit coat. Very flustered, he claimed he had forgotten al about it. The official told him they would keep for him until he came back to Moscow, and he could pick it up on his way out of the U.S.S.R!

After going through my wallet and bags, they took me into another room where the Customs man -asked me to empty my pockets, and then he (patted me down) felt my clothes up and down my body, for hidden possessions (I think!) and told me to wait there! He went out of the room, and another man came in. He asked me to unzip-and-open my pants, and he felt around my waistband -- and then he pulled my shorts forward -- and even looked into my shorts! It was so humorous -that I couldn't keep -from laughing. And I complimented him on doing such a thorough job. He gave me a sheepish smile, and declined the cigar I offered him in a gesture of friendship. I thought these people were beyond corruption, until another, higher official walked past us as we were waiting for the others to be inspected, and this official remarked how he wished he could get an umbrella for his wife, when he heard we were from the U.S. The woman standing next to me told him to step outside, where it wouldn't look improper, and she would give him one. A minute later, he came walking by me with the umbrella (a folding, convertible type.) They only checked about a quarter of the group, and that took about another 40 minutes. Then we got on a bus and went down a road to a warehouse, where we waited for another hour, looking for lost luggage.

We got to the "Russia" Hotel about 10:30 P.M., and everyone was tired and cold. After getting our rooms and washing up, we had supper at 11:00 P.M. The man I was assigned a room with, Richard Tashjian, from Boston, had been to Moscow before. He said he was an artist, and was taking acrylic paints to Yerevan to give to the artists. He asked me if I'd like to see Red Square; so we walked about four blocks to Lenin's tomb. There were two guards, standing like Statues, in front of the tomb -- and I swear, I stared at them for minutes, and couldn't even see them breathe. Another soldier was walking back-and-forth on the sidewalk, and you could tell by the smile on his face that he was humored with our curiosity of wondering whether they were statues. We couldn't communicate extensively with him because of our language barrier, and as we departed, signaling goodbye, I felt regretful --- realizing that I had traveled across an ocean and couldn't even communicate with another individual, because we assume everyone should know English. We returned to the hotel, and I went to bed at 1:30 A.M.

September 7th, 1971 -- Tuesday:
I woke up at 7:00 A.M. and my roommate "Hrratch" and I went out to take pictures, before 8:00, and were surprised to see so many tourists out so early. I had breakfast at 8:30 -- and sent a few postcards home. We got on the bus to go to the airport, and had to wait 15 minutes for the two idiots who felt like taking a tour of Moscow in a taxi! It took an hour and 20 minutes, by bus, to get to the airport. (I guess that's one of the drawbacks of having large, and ancient cities --- you have no room left to make accommodations for future conveniences. Then again, I guess it's better that way, You get a better picture of what life was like in ancient times.) As we were flying out of Moscow, you could see the shanty towns around the fringe of the city. (We may not be

proud of our impoverished slums, but we certainly don't keep it a secret. ---- And they say everyone lives in one class, there, in Communism?!) I wondered how their wheels of progress can turn so slowly, when they don't have as much red--tape to go through, as we have?! -- I know they have a manpower shortage, because I saw women mixing and carrying cement and lumber, right alongside the men, in Moscow. It seems they don't want the people to have any more than necessary. -- After seeing what affluency has done to our country (U.S. and the loss of our social order and morals) -- maybe their way is better. -- Time will tell.

We left Moscow by a 4-engine propeller-plane, to Yerevan. The plane's crew was completely Armenian ---- and you could see the difference in the attitudes of people, more talkative, and the stewardesses, more cheerful -- now we felt more at home. The trip took 3 1/2 hours, but it was a lot noisier, and you could feel the difference in the cabin pressure, how it plugged your ears up. As we flew over "our" Mt Ararat, we were told not to take any pictures, it was forbidden; bringing you back to the reality of the Soviet regime! ---- Mt Ararat -- where Noah's Ark landed -- the site of Armenia's origin -- 17,000 feet high -- reaching toward the heavens -- still pleading to God for justice of the Armenian genocide perpetrated by the Turks -- still waiting for the cruel. and unjust world to return Our lands, to the "Armenians'" (Too bad Armenians weren't in the movie making business, for then, we could be reminding the amnesia- minded world about our "Genocide," the loss of half of our Armenian race, just like the Jews who keep reminding the world about their "holocaust" in practically every movie' --- And they, ironically, are the ones who support the Turkish government, because they gave the Jews a home, centuries back, when the rest of the world was driving them out of their countries. ---- But, what about the hypocrisy -- the double standards regarding humanity -- do they forget about the suffering of Armenians because they are not "Jewish?!" -- Or can that be overlooked more easily, because we are "Christians?!!" -- Is it possible that may be the reason why the world still shuns Jews --- because the Jews isolate themselves from the world by staying in their own shells, giving the world a complex that they are contaminating the Jews with their own religious beliefs?! God help us! ---- And yet, conversely -- the "Christian" nations are no less innocent -- for wasn't it the Christian nations - the superpowers - who forgot about the Armenian nation, and the restoration of their lands?! USA -- Britain -- France --- who got tired of the "Armenian Question" and gradually forgot about them -- who later paid the consequences of their forgetfulness -- by having Hitler laugh in their allied faces! -- And the Jews suffering the "Holocaust," because the world couldn't be bothered about the Armenians!! --- One would think that the Jews would be more concerned of that reality, and if not to persuade the Turks to give Armenians their lands back, that they would distance themselves from Turkey because of their "human rights" violations -- the vanguard of all "civilized" people! Hypocrisy - hypocrisy! The price will always be paid for it! ---------

We arrived in Yerevan at 6:35 P.M., Armenia time. As we disembarked, I couldn't believe how people could react like a bunch of starving cattle, pushing to get to the trough. You would think the plane was going to take off before we could all get off! --- Ah, humanity! There were people rushing to get to the plane, to greet their relatives, with flowers in their hands. (And I'm sure these were the privileged few, who had connections to the "Party," for it seemed the commoners were still standing behind the fence, with looks of despair on their faces.) 'There was a lot of joyous tears and hugging transpiring, and I, looking to see if I Could recognize any of my relatives, for I hadn't told them the exact time of arrival, because I didn't know, and didn't want to inconvenience them for nothing. I didn't see any of my relatives at the fence, as I paced back and forth a couple of times -- and I noticed how anxiously and solemnly they were looking for people they were expecting. -- So, jokingly (just to create some laughter) I said: (in Armenia, of course: "Isn't there anyone here looking for me?" The people smiled, and someone asked me where we were from. -- And I said-- "America." And another voice in the crowd, in a forceful tone, yelled out: "Which, 'America?'" -- And I said-- "Detroit!" --- And someone in the crowd said they knew someone in 'San Francisco.' I guess they had no idea how far 'Frisco' was from Detroit!   As an afterthought, when I thought about that man's voice, who said: "Which America?!" I felt offended, feeling he was pro communist, trying to put the United States down. -- But after considerable thought, I came to the conclusion that, although I wasn't pleased with the tone of voice, I realized that there could be people, in the other "Americas," who have a right, or could feel a sense of indignation for overlooking them as Americans! So that man -- as much as I detested Communism -- did me a favor of enlightening me to my erroneous concept, and made me more considerate of our two other Americas. So, Canadians, Central Americans, and South Americans -- Forgive me , eg. "pardone moi", "scuse mi muchachos", and "scusatami ignorante Americani"! We "Americans" can't possibly realize how these poor people yearn to see someone they're related to -- especially, "Americayeets!" After about an hour at the airport, we finally got our luggage on the bus and got to the "Ani." Hotel at 8:00 P.M. -- where we spent 45 minutes in the lobby before we got to our rooms, because of the bad elevator and poor reservation facilities at the hotel. (They tried to pair up two people to a room, and fortunately, since I was not from California, and was not with my wife, I had the good fortune to be assigned to a room by myself. Another thing that they did, which was so obtrusive was, they assigned us to different floors, scattering us apart, and I imagine it was for the deliberate purpose of allowing the female desk clerk - which they had on each floor - the opportunity to more easily familiarize themselves with us, individually. It was definitely a burglar-proof system -- for every time you left your room, you would leave your key with her, at the desk -- and she would hand it to you upon returning, when you got off of the elevator, even before you said your name! --- And I'm sure, if anything was stolen from your room --"she" would be held responsible! And I never heard anyone say they were missing anything. We had supper at 9:05 P.M., and the dining room was very large and palatial; but, I was disappointed when they served us chicken. (Last 4 meals!)

Later, I walked around town and saw the Russian Arts Building. When I came back to the hotel, I asked the doorman if he had heard of the street my aunt lived on, and he said he had never-heard of it. Then I asked a cab driver, and he said he had driven a cab for eight years and never heard of such a street. I asked a few more people, including the hotel receptionist, and she very sarcastically suggested I seek information at the "registration" office, in town. (My aunt's street was less than a mile from the hotel.) Had the receptionist known I was an American, I'm certain she would not have been sarcastic, but it showed me how critically they treat their own people! "Authority," in the Soviet Union really goes to the heads of those who belong to the party. It's ironic what kind of reactions your attire may get you when you travel in foreign countries.--- If I had a suit on I'm certain the receptionist would have smiled at me! -- But it reminds me of the time when I walked out of a hotel in Rome, wearing a suit and tie, and had just lit a cigar, when I went walking past a fruit stand, and this woman peddler yelled "Fascista" at me!! --- "Me," a Fascist??! ---- I had been smoking cigars since I graduated from high school at 17, and bought my first cigar after my first pay check from work, and then a steelworker most of my life. --- And just because I was wearing a suit and tie, smoking a cigar, she calls me a "Fascist!" I only wished I could have spoken Italian --(and I don't mean the profanity)-- I would have told her I'm a Christian, a hard working man, and I love her like a brother, and would have asked her why she hated me, without even knowing me!

The droning' of the airplane, and the frustrations must have given me a headache, so I went to my room and unpacked my clothes -- then I took a shower and went to bed at 1.00 A.M. Three things I couldn't help notice in the bathroom: (1) the toilet water wouldn't stop completely (2) that they don't use shower curtains, or doors -- the floors are tiled, with a drain in the middle of the bathroom (3) make sure you put the light on in the bathroom at night or you'll have waterbugs all over the floor, that come out of the floor drain when it's dark!

September 8th, Wednesday:
Woke up at 4.00 A.M. to the sounds of a scraping noise --(since it was hot and I had left the window open.) I wondered what kind of noise that could possibly be at this time of night -- and when I looked out the window, I saw an elderly woman sweeping the street -- I really should say "scraping." -- She had a "broom" that may have been as ancient as brooms when "brooms" were originated! It was a tree- limb with a bunch of twigs tied to the end of it. I didn't know if they intended to sweep the streets clean or scrape them clean, they made so much noise-- (and I'm riot a light sleeper). The water trucks sprayed water and the woman swept the streets every night. Hey, make all the noise you want -- I love clean streets! The streets were clean, but the Armenians would litter the streets more than the Russians in Moscow!

I couldn't sleep, so I turned up the volume (no on/off switches on radios in hotels, here -- I thought it could be used as a two-way microphone conversation-detection, but, then again, it could be a cheaper way of not replacing switches - since the electricity is free. I was no spy, so why should I worry.) The sound on the radio seemed like large, church bells ringing -- announcing the time -- it was now 5:00 A.M. About five minutes later, the streetlights went out. It gets fairly light at this time. The radio was now playing what sounded like "Anchors Aweigh" and it seemed unusual to hear a Russian woman's voice marking-time that sounds like 1-2-3-4 and I Couldn't imagine anyone doing ballet at this time of the day?! (Later, when I told my mother about this, she laughed, and said they were "exercising!" Who-da-hell. is going to be exercising at this time of the morning?')

The radio is a one-station radio! (Now that did confirm my suspicions.) The toilet water was running and gurgling all night. I tried to go back to sleep, and as I laid there listening to the radio, the Russian program went off of the air, and an Armenian voice came on (now 6:00 A.M.) -- broadcasting from the one-and-only radio station in town! At 7:00 A.M., I was still awake, So I got up and shaved, got dressed and went out looking for the "Registration Office." As I headed in the direction of the office, I couldn't help but be curious as to what they had in the grocery stores, as I looked at the people and the way the were dressed, and what they bought, and the prices. I couldn't help notice how they had lined up at the meat counters, waiting their turn to purchase meat. Everything was chopped-up at the moment of request -- nothing lying around to spoil. I asked a male customer in the store, who was buying bread, how much he paid for, loaf. He asked me where I was from -- then, when he found out what I was looking for, he took me to, and into, the Registrar's office. The woman in charge asked me my name, my aunt's name and address, and within two minutes of index-file searching, she told me exactly where it was.

    I returned to the hotel for breakfast -- thinking I would visit my aunt after I ate. And after washing up in my room, I was coming down the stairs to the dining--room lobby (seems the Soviet Union doesn't believe having an elevator stop on their 2nd floor dining rooms -- probably for theft protection purposes). And as I entered the stairway, I saw my Uncle "Marklen" (my mother's brother) at the same time he saw me, and within a moment we recognized each other. Cousin Yura was with him, also. He had a quizzical look at first, that changed to surprise, and then to happiness!! I half yelled, "Marklen" in a joyous tone, and went bounding down the steps -- two--and-three at a time. I jumped down the flight so fast that I thought I was worried I was going to shove him through the wall when I grabbed him, wrapping my arms around him and hugging and kissing him, with tears pouring from our eyes, half-laughing and crying from years of pent up yearnings, with me saying "morr-yeghpyrr" ("mother's- brother": meaning, "uncle".)

It seemed the world stopped turning in that minute's time and God had allowed me the fulfillment of my lifelong dream of seeing my uncle -- and relatives. I had been writing to them for years, and waiting for what seemed like a hundred generations, never seriously thinking I would be able to see him in person. Then Yura and I hugged each other, and kissed. My cousin; long lost cousins I never knew before. I mean "real" cousins that I never dreamed I'd ever see. "Cousins" I always envied other people of. -- My relatives!

I didn't stay for breakfast -- it seemed the hotel didn't allow non-guests to dine in the restaurant -- and I certainly didn't want to have them wait until I ate -- although they urged me to, and since I was eager to see my aunt, I told them: "Let's go.!" Uncle Marklen caught a cab and we went to his sister's house -- Yura's mother -- my mother's youngest sister, whom I also had been writing to for years. My aunt "Ovsanna," who's house I was trying to find, a mile from the hotel.

The streets were in good shape, until we got nearer to my aunts area, and then it seemed the roads were under repair, holes, here and there. As we approached the base of a very large hill, where a road began to run up alongside the hill, my uncle told the cabby to turn off to the right, at the base of the hill, and into an area that was paved with cement. (Although it was supposed to be a street, it seemed that the area was built from excess cement that may have been left over from other contract jobs, and they had just dumped it there and leveled it off as they went along. The side of the hill, where the road ran up it, was braced with rocks and blocks and more excess cement. -- It either seemed that way, or it was really a shoddy job of road repair work. -- I never asked. -- But as I found out later from my cousin, he said the government wanted to eliminate the area, because it was an eyesore of patchwork homes, and were informing the residents not to keep building, that they intended to tear the homes down and move them into new apartments. --- But, it seemed the people that were coming into town to live didn't give a damn what they were being told, they just kept on building. -- It seemed the whole Soviet system was a "rip-off" -- the government ripping-off the masses, and the masses ripping-off the government, especially those who were the laborers! --- And I can't say that I could blame them. --- The elite "party" members, who had the better jobs -- directing and supervising the laborers, lived off of the sweat of the laborers, and the laborers would rip off the government by taking home any piece of equipment or material they could lay their hands on! - And it seemed that's how the city of Yerevan was being constructed on the fringes. The inner city was well planned, modern, and quite spacious -- just as other major cities in the Soviet process. -- But there were boring, redundant similarities of apartment and office building construction, with the same drab gray colors, sizes and shapes. -- They lacked the personalities of human creativity --- which obviously lacked the expression of freedom's air! - And that unquestionably, to me, seemed to infect the psyche of the Soviet citizen! -- They didn't seem to exude the sense of carefree happiness, as people possess in free Countries! -- If there was "happiness" -- it was a self-generated, forced-happiness, because the people knew they were still, programmed robots living like "prisoners" in their own land! And what made it worse than the mentality of a "criminal"-prisoner is that a criminal knows he is going to be released after he serves his term!

This was where my aunt Ovsanna lived -- at the bottom of the hill -- where everyone referred to as "sarree-tagh" -- "the area of the mountain." -- I wouldn't call it a Mountain, but it was high enough where you could overlook the whole city! And it seemed the city was surrounded on three sides with these large hills, and opening toward the "plains" to the South. Yerevan seemed to be built in a valley -- and well laid out, architecturally.

As we got out of the cab and started walking toward aunt Osvanna's house, I saw a few people standing in the doorway. Aunt Ovsanna (who was about 51) ran out to greet me, with my uncle's wife, "Tamara," right behind her! I recognized them from the pictures that she had sent me over the years --- but it was mostly of her sons, two sisters, and "Marietta," who was her sister's granddaughter, whom I also had corresponded with. ---- We hugged and kissed -- with more tears being shed, and they both walked me, arm-in-arm, to the house, and my other aunts and cousins hugged and kissed me, with more tears flowing.

(I Must say here, dear reader, that you should try to envision yourself in my place, and remember: you've never known what it's like to have anyone other than your parents, brothers and sisters in your life, and a few days short of being 45 years old. Hearing stories from your mother about her youth, as being the oldest offspring in her family. Describing the Georgian village of "Shoulaver" that she came from, and her father's livelihood as a merchant, coming from a family of "15" (more on this later) and leaving home at 17 after being tricked into marrying my father. --- And then, with my wife, coming from a family with so many relatives around Detroit and not getting excited about that fact. -- And me, wondering what it would be like to have "relatives" and what life could have been like if I had lived in Armenia, or Georgia, with my loving Armenian relatives. --- And then, to realize some of your Armenian dreams ---- it was too overwhelming, the emotions tear your heart apart! And there were times when I felt my heart was really going to burst from the love and tribulations that were heaped on me! --- You'll notice, I said: realizing "some" of my Armenian dreams --- for- my grandparents were all dead before I got there -- and my paternal grandmother had starved to death because of the Turks, just like my mother-in-laws whole family getting annihilated by the Turkish perpetrated genocide! --- And to think of half the Armenian population, 1,457,251 people being killed or starved to death by the Turks --- and then 50 years of Communist rule over the remaining 1,500,000 Armenians -- wondering when they would ever regain freedom again -- or the restoration of Armenian territory from the Turks. ---- Imagine how you would feel, dear reader?!)

Then I Met Yura's brother Jura, and his wife Maretta and two children, who were all living in the same house. As if the emotions weren't enough to cope with, there were so many relatives and so many names, I was overwhelmed trying to remember the names and the relationships --- and this was just the beginning.
We sat around the dining room table, talked and drank Cognac and "rahkhi" "whiskey" (home made) while breakfast was being made, and after breakfast -- which was something of a rarity for me, for mornings. While talking with my cousin Yura, he asked me why I was feeling bad (tears in my eyes,) and I told him how it saddened me to see the condition they were existing in. He told me not to feel sorry for them that, they were living pretty good and asked me to follow him, and he'd show me something. -- We went down about 7 stairs, under the house. They were in the process of fixing up the house and making additions to it, and he said they were going to finish off the place into a basement. He showed me the outline of a six-foot-square piece of concrete and told me there used to be four walls around that piece of concrete, with a board on top of it, which was as high as the basement (meaning the ground, outside). And he said; "This used to be our home, so you see, we're living good now -- so don't feel sorry for us." When he pointed to that six-foot square, I really broke up. I'M sure he was sincere in trying to dispel my heartache. -- After I was there for a while, I had to agree that my cousin was right-- everything is relevant. -- Although I don't feel as bad about it, I still feel sorry for them, and will never forget!

Accompanied by some of my relatives, I went back to the hotel around noon. It was about 100 degrees F. today, but the humidity must be lower, because you don't perspire as much. We washed up, and then I took my suitcase back to aunt Ovsanna's house. The suitcase was laden with gifts from everyone back home. We had dinner and more cognac, and near the end of dinner, my uncle (my father's brother) came walking in. I had never seen my paternal uncle before - or even a "picture" of him - but the moment I saw him, I knew it was my father's brother ("Avo"). He looked just like him! ---- My father had died in 1949 -- 22 years ago -- at the age of 61 -- and my uncle was 14 years younger than him, which makes him about 70 today. It was like seeing my father again --- so you can imagine how I felt!! We hugged each other, and I really cried, and him along with me. --- 'There were so many of them --- and they had each other all those years -- but "me," I had no relatives to talk to -- and yet, I never thought how "they" must have felt. - Were their yearnings as strong for "me," as mine, for them?! --- But I didn't realize how much they could love "me"' ---(more later, on that.) Boy, my uncle was really torn up. -- He wasn't just crying, he was sobbing -- and I think it was a close match between me and-him! We were crying so hard that it may have been possible my relatives may have thought they were going to have to build an ark, like 'Noah's.' It was a grieving kind of sob --- like he had waited 50 years just to see me. Everyone there, was in tears!! (He told me, later, that he was 14 years old when my father left home.) I guess his hurt was even worse than mine, since I looked like my father.

Later in the afternoon, he had his sister's daughter and her son, David ("Daveet") come over, with David's wife Svetanna) and we ate and drank some more. Uncle Marklen, my cousins and I went for a walk around town. They showed me the large farmer's market (and referred to it as "Betagon" market, because it was controlled by the state. And those farmers who had their own, separate fruit stands were referred as "Sepagon.") I was surprised that the communists allowed that, but then, I guess it was another method of inducing-farmers to be more productive and reassuring a larger share of produce. We were comparing theirs to US prices and I felt theirs were about equal to ours, or even higher. And to think their average worker makes abut $100.00 a month'! And that's 5 days per week, at 7 hours a day -- which comes to 71 cents an hour. Yet, we (USA) complain about not being able to make ends meet! Then we went to the hotel later, to see if they would allow me to go to Kirovagan, uncle Marklen's city. They had him fill out a form requesting permission to take me, and told him to check with them the next day, for approval. (Well, it doesn't take long to see how the Soviet-system works -- and it sure isn't a free society. It seems everyone is in charge of your life -- directing you on how you must live -- and "you better be a good boy" or you don't get any more privileges!! -- It stinks! (But, being a tourist, you learn to keep your mouth shut, and follow orders. Not only because they can send you right back home on the next plane, or you don't want to create problems for your own State Department if in the event they send you to Siberia, but mainly, because you don't want to cause any problems for your relatives!) When we got back to Aunt Ovsanna's house, I had a feeling my paternal uncle's feelings were hurt, because, as I found out later, we had been gone for a few hours. It wasn't that I acted totally ignorant by neglecting him, it was just that I was trying to be accommodating to Uncle Marklen, and also felt it would give them time to acquaint themselves. I didn't know, at the time, that they were from two different-sides of the "fence." -- So, in retrospect, I imagine it could have caused a strained conversation.

We had supper, and the cognac started to flow again. Everyone was making a toast to me. -- More relatives came from out of town. Davit, my second cousin, and his wife came again -- obviously, invited back for dinner.

They kept toasting me for hours, with cognac,."rahkhi" (whiskey) and "geenee" (wine) - and I was feeling the effects of the cognac. But, more than the effect of the cognac, were my thoughts about their plight and deprivation -- the 2nd World War that had taken my other-uncles, leaving their widows and children behind -- and the living conditions they had to endure under the "Soviet" regime.

It was humiliating to me, when they showered me with love and affection, without reservation. -- It was something that I had never experienced before -- all this attention; it made me feel so humble.

The combination of seeing my father's brother, who was sitting at my side, with my mother's brother at my other side, made me aware that my coming here had brought both sides together for-the-first-time-- from different cities. - Uncle Avo was from Leninakan, who lived near his sister, but Davit and his mother lived in Yerevan. I thought about how my father and his brother were separated from the time my uncle was 14 years old, and how he had to take care of himself. -- All this had such an overwhelming, emotional effect on me that I couldn't stop crying. I was numb, mentally and physically. Maybe it was a good thing I was sedated with alcohol, for I honestly believe I could have gone over the edge of sanity!! Only a person who has experienced lifelong thoughts as mine, and experienced what I experienced there, at that gathering, could possibly understand that possibility!! -- It was like being torn between Heaven and hell!
We took a cab back to the Hotel Ani. Because it was late, my relatives wanted to see me to my room.
It was past midnight, and the doorman had a cable around the door handles and made sure a person was registered at the hotel, before letting them in.
I threw up about 1:00 A.M. and took a couple of aspirins before going back to bed.

September 9th, Thursday:
Morning hangover! -- Woke up at 8.OO A.M., shaved, showered, got dressed and went down to the lobby. There was uncle Marklen and cousins Yura, and Shura-from-Tiflis, Georgia. (Boy, trying to remember names and faces were bad enough -- but the

names of my cousins: Yura, Jhura, Jhora and Shura were quite perplexing.) I thought I was up early, and these guys are here, waiting for me. We went walking around town and visited more shops, upon my request. Then we went to Aunt Ovsan's (short for Ovsanna - which was what they called her) and uncle Avo (my father's brother) was there. We took some pictures out in front of the house. We had breakfast, and as usual, more cognac. (I think I'm becoming an alcoholic!) That afternoon, we took a bus to the small town of Etchmiadzin, which is the residence of our "Catholicos" (like the Pope, at the Vatican) and the Holy Cathedral of the Armenian Church, built in 303 AD -- one year after Armenians adopted Christianity as a State religion. I always thought Etchmiadzin was the name of the Cathedral. Now, today, I realized they named it after the Holy City, for, "Etchmiadzin" means: "Where God set down." (Literally, Etchmiadzin ="descent, The Only Begotten," --- or to that intent. I'm not an expert.)

The drivers on the roads can be hazardous. If you took the horns off of their cars, I think the drivers would be lost --they're really horn-crazy -- worse than Italians.

Drinking water flows constantly from fountains at different points on the premises, and there are various monuments on the grounds, which are enclosed by walls on all sides. The Cathedral was, being repaired on the outside by men working on scaffolds, and taking directions from a man on the ground. The whole structure seemed to be constructed with cut, grey stone. The first thing that catches your eye is the huge chandelier in the main part of the Cathedral, directly in front of the Bema (Altar.) It is about 8 feet high and 5 1/2 feet wide, and made of crystal. Considering the year it was built, it is fairly good sized. I lit two candles in memory of Simon and Bedros (my father, and father-in-law) and thanked God for allowing me this opportunity. The right and left wings of the Cathedral were decorated with icon paintings of the apostles. Flashbulbs were necessary to take good pictures inside. We saw a display of ancient Bibles and manuscripts, coins, large hand-sewn rugs -that hung from the wall, and other interesting collections, too numerous to mention, that were in rooms built in back of the Altar. It took less than 1/2 an hour to drive back to Yerevan.

We walked around town. -- There was a street urchin begging for money, with her mother, and they were dressed like nomads. Uncle Avo raised the back-of-his-hand to her and criticized her for begging! My uncle Marklen's wife, Tamara gave the mother some money. -- That's the difference in Communist subjects --- pro - and - con!

We sat by the "Boulevard of Fountains" - there were 2,750 water-pipes protruding from the shallow pool -- one pipe for each year of Yerevan's age --- and water continually sprays from them. We went back to Ovsanna's house and had dinner. The liquor started flowing again, with more toasts to me. They are really professionals at making toasts. Each individual speaks, for minutes -- and it seemed as if they were trying to outdo each other. Here it was -- 2 weeks short of my 45 birthday -- and I had never, never heard such orations at toasting a person -- especially to me, which had never happened before. But the toasts were in memory of loved ones who had passed-on, and lamentations of regrets that they couldn't be here for this occasion, to have seen "Sooren!" I was really impressed, but more than that, I was envious -- that I couldn't have made toasts like that. But, then again, I never had the training program, like these guys. -- I liked to drink, but sociably, and only on special occasions, or parties. But these guys were "professionals" -- and I was out of my league! --- Of course, if I lived under communist oppression, I undoubtedly would have been as good as them, for there is no outlet for their frustration. It seemed all the men were professional imbibers!! And the poor wives had to suffer more than the men, because they not only had to empathize with their spouse's frustration, but also with their alcohol problems. That's why there are so many alcoholics in the Soviet Union.

They sang, more food, more toasts. They passed out the gifts that I had brought. They really got excited about the chewing gum; even, the grown-ups! (You'll see why, later.) The kids were passing the one stick of gum from mouth to-mouth, for hours!! And the parents didn't even give it a second thought. --- And we get fanatical about germs in the States?! And they looked like healthy kids to "me!"

We went back to the hotel about 1:00 A.M. and I took a shower and went to bed.

September 10th, Friday
Uncle Marklen called about 7:30 A.M. and said they were in the lobby with another relative, from Shoulaver, "Verastan" (Georgia, in Armenian language.) I shaved and dressed, and ran down 4 flights of stairs -- (I got tired of waiting for the cantankerous elevator) -- to see a one-armed man with my uncle and his family waiting in the lobby. It was another cousin of mine! We hugged and kissed, (as usual in Armenia) and tears came to his eyes. Due to the war and dire circumstances, most of my cousins were left fatherless!

Uncle Marklen took us to breakfast -- in a separate dining area of the hotel. It was the first time I had eggs since I left home, and the table was overflowing with food. And guess what?! Cognac, again! Can you see me drinking four double-shots for breakfast?! Uncle Marklen, the day before at his sister Ovsan's house, asked me who drank the most in our family. (I have 2 older brothers, and I younger.) I told him: "'Me' -- but I had more to drink in my first three days in Yerevan than I had in the last three years!" He held his thumb up with a closed fist and said: "Hey, You drink pretty good!" They finished the rest of the cognac. What food they served! Nothing like the "tourists'" dining room, on the other side of the hotel. We had smoked fish that tasted like smoked ham, and ground veal, shaped like dolma (stuffed cabbage) and it was breaded and deep--fried (?) and really good.

My paternal uncle, Avo was supposed to pick me up this noon at 1:00 P.M. to visit our Apkarian-side of the family, but I had to go sightseeing! The girl (22) in charge of our tour was really upset that I hadn't been showing up for the tours, and was almost in tears. She said I had no business going anywhere without first being excused by the government or until, after I had gone sightseeing. She told me that the only reason she hadn't complained to the officials was because of my politeness and manners. My uncle Marklen was still trying to convince her about letting me be excused, while at the same time one of the other tourists was giving her a hard time about his absence, when an official came over and wanted to know what the problem was. After he found out, my uncle asked him if we could be excused; the tourist started giving him (official) some back-talk about being an American, and was able to do what he wanted. (This younger guy was from Detroit, whom I knew, since he was related to my in-laws --- and when he was back in the "States" he used to tell every body how good Communism was, while he worked at the US Post Office! But now, he's claiming he's an "American citizen." 'Huh!') The official became angered and told my uncle I couldn't be excused. He also told us, that if we broke the rules we could be sent back to the USA -- and asked: "Do you understand?!" (in Armenian.) I was apologetic, in explaining our misunderstanding, because I would rather be a credit to the USA, and a goodwill Ambassador. -- But, "Joe," this other guy, from Detroit -- kept mouthing-off and saying-. "You don't scare me!" The official got angered to the point that seemed, to me, he was going to take immediate, drastic action. I stepped-in and told the jerk, that if he didn't give a damn about the money he had spent, then he should at least show enough concern for the pleasure of his elderly parents, who he was supposed to be looking after, on this trip, and not spoil their-fun. (I had heard stories before, about the harsh treatment others had received when not following orders, and I knew they would have sent him back!!

Upon the official's suggestion, uncle Marklen went to the Regulation Desk to fill out a form of approval, for excusing me from the tour, so that I would be able to go to Kirovagan. (When we got back from the sightseeing trip to Erebuni, they said the request was denied.) My second trip to Erebuni, with the sightseeing trip was more informative and appreciated than when my relatives took me. -- So I can understand why they want you to go with the tour - although, I'm certain their ulterior motive was to make sure we had nicer things to say about our trip in order to encourage more visitors, and "American dollars."

When we got back to the hotel, my uncle Avo was there with his niece, (Davit's mother) "Shooshig" (about age 59?) We embraced and kissed, and my uncle got tears in his eyes, which caused a chain reaction upon me. Both of my uncles were there, and it seemed as if they must have had some differences of some sort as to where I was supposed to go. Uncle Marklen told me to go with uncle Avo. -- As we were to depart, uncle Marklen asked Avo what time we'd be back. -- And his answer was, 9:00 P.M.. (I felt uncomfortable being the subject of creating problems. -- And although I didn't want to be led around like I didn't have any desires of my own, I was still willing to overlook my own pleasures just to bring them all the happiness I could. Although I had never written letters to Uncle Avo, and didn't know anything about his side of the family, since my father hardly ever had spoken about it, except with my mother. I not only wanted to learn more about the "Apkarian" side, but I wanted to show him the respect that he deserved, since he was, elderly. (Now I could see how the Soviet authority is wielded around, just by the subtle tones of authority that are expressed among my relatives -- but, during non-relative conversations -- they were more. authoritatively outspoken!) And my Uncle Marklen was a barber --- so, you could see he didn't have any "party" affiliations' -- Although, I'm certain, he held respect for elderly folks, like Uncle Avo.

Just from first impressions, not only of speech or dress, you can detect the importance of people by the dignified elegance they exude. -- And my cousin, "Shooshig" had that air of dignity. (As I learned later, I was right, she was a doctor!)

We got to Shooshig's place, which was less than a mile from the hotel, in the opposite direction of town from where Aunt Ovsanna lived, and it was in an elevated area of rolling hills -- only, solid rock. The houses in Yerevan looked like they are from 40 to 70 years old. The government is in the process of eliminating them, and compelling people to move into apartment complexes. Half of the town is in a transitory stage. There are apartments going up all over the place. It seems they are biting off more than they can chew. I noticed the greater majority of steel structures were standing idle, without further activity of laborers in sight. But, there's no question about progress being made. They claim a drastic manpower shortage. From what I observed, they do a sloppy job of building-construction, compared to our standards. -- If they were built -as well as their monuments, they'd be Superb!

Shooshig's place was a very old, two-storied flat, but very nicely taken care of. We spoke in quiet tones, wondering what to say, and as if there was a baby sleeping -- and there was. Cousin Shooshig introduced me to her 3 girls and her sister-in-law. We spoke, and I answered their questions. They were very-well mannered and refined people. It was an altogether, different atmosphere than at Ovsan's--- quiet and peaceful --- no children screaming, no noisy traffic going by. Her son, Davit (age 33) came home from work. His mother asked him if he was going to shave his day's growth, before supper. (The men probably shave 2 or 3. times a week, there. They were surprised to hear that I shave about 370) times a year. ---(In the steel-mill, years back, I used to work with an older guy named Tommy O'Donnell -- and when he told me he shaved every day, that's when I told myself: "If he can do it, so can I." I wanted to-be a clean-cut looking guy, like him! And on special occasions, I'd even shave twice a day.)

After Davit shaved, he started a large, wooden-fire in the backyard, on the ground. They roasted large chunks of lamb (without removing the bones, as we do in the States.) And they don't prefer "shish-kebob" to their way of making it, which they call, "Khorrovahdz" (which means "roast"-- not the Turkish terminology, "kebab"! -- and shish - pronounced "sheesh"-- the skewer, in Turkish, is called "shampiure" in Armenian. So Armenians, in Armenia call shish-kabob -- "Shampiure-ov-khorrovadz!" Roast-with-a-skewer. No Turkish words HERE. They had whole tomatoes, peppers and eggplants on very large skewers. We took a few pictures in the yard. They really had set a fine and dignified table --- a radical transition from the "haves" and "have-nots" --- from the non--party to the party side of the fence. -- It was like two different worlds. (But then -- we've got the same extremes in the US !! -- The only difference is, you can get rich in the US, from your own sweat -- if you want to!) But, Armenians are all earthy people. -- Maybe it's because those that live a better life never forget where they came from! We drank, spoke for a while, and the Russian lady's husband came in and dined.   We later went to "Yegherrnee" (monument of "atrocity"-- the monument that was built in memory of the 1,547,231 Armenians that perished from the "Genocide" perpetrated by the villainous Turks during 1915 - 1920. A period in time where wild animals rose from hell and annihilated every Armenian they possibly could -- because they were "Christians" -- and the "Civilized" world turned its eyes so as not to witness the horror that they didn't want to account-to- God, for!! Woe to those beasts, Enver and Tallat Pasha! And also those neutral nations that stood idly by and allowed this heinous crime on the civilization of Armenia. For, as Jesus said; "Whatever you did for the least of them, you also did unto me"! Woe - woe - woe!! Jesus --- our Christ! And Armenians died like sacrificial lambs, because the Turks, just as the ancient Persians, could not take our Christianity away from us without our supreme sacrifice, like, Jesus.

My 2nd-cousin, Davit told me that the old man, who was eating dinner with us, had built the monument with his own hands! It was a dual-structured monument. To the right was a square-shaped spire that was about 15 feet across at the base, and rose to a point at about a height of 150 feet. The structure to the left was Circular in shape, with a base of about 100 feet in diameter, and tapered at the top to about 75 feet in diameter, and rose to a height of about 25 feet. It was about 9 sectional pieces, with about 5-foot spaces between each piece, and possibly 6 feet thick. I think the designer may have been trying to reflect the image of a volcano, for, as I entered the structure, the floor slanted downward toward the center, where there was a hole with a flame coming out of it, and it was ringed off with a large chain. The effect of the design, and the memory-for-which it was built, sure, touched me. --- As I stood there looking at the flame, I felt as if I was standing in the core of the Earth, and mother-nature was releasing her- "flame of souls" from all the dead Armenians she had consumed. Although, grievously sad, it was the most tranquil feeling I have ever had in my life.

We chatted extensively, as we walked around there, and then took a taxi back to the inner city. Davit said: "Keetchum frrrutsnenk?" (Which inferred; "shall we take a little-bit spin" (a little spin around town). And concurrently reminded me of my father, telling me and my two older brothers, when we were kids, when he was teaching us how to spin a top! -- I hadn't heard that, "frrrutsnenk" word, in all those years! -- I guess you could say, it sort of, "brings you home!" The "nem" ending is singular, and "nenk" is plural. (Too bad the Anglos couldn't have taken a lesson from the Armenians before they contrived the English language. It would have been more simplified. Then again, I don't think they would have appreciated the 38 letters in our alphabet! But, they say our alphabet can cover any spoken language! Who needs "Esperanto?!") We returned back to Davit's house, after the "spin,"-- and Uncle Avo was sitting there, quietly. We spoke for another hour-and-a-half, and at 10:00 P.M., when it was suggested we return to the hotel for his 9:00 P.M. promise, Uncle Avo said: "Let them wait." Since- he was much older, and had less time to spend with me, I didn't say anything to hurt his feelings. At 11:20 P.M. we walked back to the hotel (that'll make sure we return later) and they came up to look at my room (and maybe to see the inside of the hotel.) I think he was deliberately infringing on Uncle Marklen's time (and once again, I witnessed the dominating attitude of the Communist party!) My Uncle Marklen wasn't there. And my paternal relatives left at 11:00 P.M. The phone rang at 11:30, and Uncle Marklen said they had been at the hotel and didn't see us. He said they'd be over in the morning, before I went on a tour, at 10:00 A.M. I washed a few articles of clothing, took a shower, and went to bed at 1:30 A.M.

September 11th, Saturday
I got up at 7:00 AM, straightened out my washed clothes, and the phone rang at 7:30. Uncle Marklen was downstairs, with his sister Ovsanna, and I told him I'd be down in 10 minutes. I shaved and dressed, and met them in the lobby. Uncle Marklen wanted to take me to breakfast, but I told him it would be a waste not to eat my hotel meal, and that I had to go with the tour to "Sevan-a-Lege"--Lake Sevan. The bus ride to Sevan was about 1-1/2 hours. We traveled over winding and bumpy roads, with the craziest driver of all -- and he really had a passion for blowing his horn'! What a beautiful countryside. Before we got there, we drove under a bird-winged-like structure, built over the highway. "Sossie" (our lady guide) told us it was a monument symbolizing Armenia's love (for peace?) About 10 minutes before we reached -the lake, it seemed as if there was an imaginary line we crossed -- for the temperature dropped from 75 to 55 (F.) in about a minute's time' You would think we drove directly into a refrigerator, after being in the sun. The lake was larger than I thought it would be! It's about 570 square miles, and the water is so cold and clean that you can drink right from the lake.

We must have walked up about 400 steps to get to the top of the hill, on the peninsula, that had an 1,100 year old small church there. At one time, not too long ago, this church used to be considered a structure on an island -- until an excessive amount of water was pumped out of it for the generation of hydroelectric power. The level dropped 6 feet, which resulted in revealing ancient, civilized structure, which was built at the lower level, before the water level rose and hid these structures for hundreds of years. They are now in the process of drilling a tunnel (about 18 miles long) through solid rock, in an attempt to fill the lake to its former level. We went for a boat-ride on the lake, and surprisingly, it was a hydroplane-boat, about 35 - 40 feet long. We had dinner at the Sevan Restaurant (the new one.) They gave us the famous "Ishkan dzoog" (Lake Sevan trout,) veal, cheese, tomatoes, salad, and wine and "lemonada." It was a delicious meal. The place was large enough to accommodate 60 - 80 people. There was another group of tourists dining there, and when we heard them orating toasts to Lake Sevan, we knew they were Scandinavians, from Norway, and we applauded them. An Armenian Musical duo came in off of the highway and sat by our table and started singing and playing the accordion and "dumbeg" (bongo type of drum.) The guy had a very good baritone voice (Sarkis Sarkisian). We sang and danced to Armenian music as the Norwegian group was leaving, and they even tried our steps. Then a polka started, and it made me feel good to see an Armenian widow, from California, dance with a Norwegian. It left me with the impression that she was dancing her cares away. We really had a good time there. When we returned to the hotel in Yerevan, my paternal Uncle--Avo was there, waiting for me -- and we went to my room. We talked for awhile, and when he asked me how his brother (my father) died (cancer, just before 62), he cried, and then I shed a few tears watching him (at age 70) cry. He said: "It's too bad he died so young -- us 'Apkarians' live to be 85 - 90 years old." He told me that he had to return to his sick wife and sister, in Tiflis (Georgia) and we hugged each other and cried again, before he entered the taxi--cab, for the train station. Words alone would not be enough to express the feeling that I was left with. To see my father's brother for the first time -- and such a striking resemblance, after 22 years of my father's death, and being so close to him -- I was, and still am, walking around in a dream. It really does something to Your Soul.

My cousins called a little later, and I went to Aunt Ovsan's house. My Uncle Marklen was "bombed-out" (drunk) and asleep on the couch. We spoke for about an hour, and then Marklen woke up. He went out and returned about half-an-hour later, with two bottles of cognac (in response to me jokingly saying, "Sure," about drinking some more, when he asked me if I wanted a drink --- especially after we overindulged a couple of nights before! Hell, I had enough to drink to last me a year. But I think this visit gave them more of an excuse to drink more -- and yet, as much as I had, and since I didn't know if I'd never see them again --- I figured, "what the hell!" -- and drank right with them -- even though I couldn't keep up! We all joined in for dinner, except Marklen -- he just ate "Ishkan" trout. He insisted that we drink -- and he got activated from the Cognac again and started singing to me in a very audible tone. He cried while he sang. It was at very unusual feeling for me - for I never had a man sing his heart out to me before! For a little guy (5' 5" 130#) he sure had a strong voice! -- Aunt Ovsan said: He's so happy, because you're here, and he's got to get it out of his system." -- He kissed me on -the forehead, on the eyes, and even on my lips!' (He did all of this as he sang.) --- In about forty-five minutes, he was sleeping it off, again. His wife "Tamara," and son "Aramais" and my cousin Yura and I went for a walk around town. Tamara said: "He normally doesn't drink much anymore, but this is a special occasion." Later, we went to the train station and saw my (blue-eyed) cousin "Shura" and his family off, for home (Shulaver.) We walked around town about 10:30 P.M. and sat on a park bench and talked some more. It was unusual to see other women walking around so late, seeming as if there wasn't anything to fear.) Tamara had bought some candy and fruit, and they came up to my hotel room. They left about 1:30 A.M. I took a bath and tried to keep my diary up to date (after missing my logging of the previous day) as I soaked my legs. I went to bed at 3:00) A.M.

September l2th, 1971: Sunday
.Woke up at 7:00 A.M. Our- tour was going to Etchmiadzin, the Holy See of all Armenian Churches in the world. (Although, prior to the "Genocide," Armenians at one time used to have three Sees (similar to Pontifical) since the Armenian terrain was too difficult to traverse and be maintained by one "Head." Although, only one was officially recognized, and subordinate to -- and with the genocidal dispersion,, where a mass of Armenians ended up in Lebanon, a second See was formulated with the election of a Second Catholicos (still subject to Etchmiadzin).--- And that didn't transpire until after the Russians usurped Armenia, into the Soviet Union!

Well, we waited for the bus in front of the hotel from 10:00 to 11:00 A.M., taking advantage of the opportunity to converse with 13 other members of our tour, who were at Hotel Armenia, an older building.

We got there a little late -- since Armenian churches begin at 11:O0 AM) -- the Service was well under way, but usually lasts 1-1/2 hrs. They ushered us right up to the front left wing. The place was really crowded. (Who said they're all atheists in the Soviet Union?!) We were right alongside the throne of His Holiness, Vasken 1. They give visitors special treatment here! The choir was exalting. The first two rows were filled with Priests from different countries. The gawkers and souvenir buyers (gold crosses and Icons) at the back of the Cathedral were disrupting the tranquility of the Service -- and it would seem it was acceptable to the church officials, for no one was trying to quiet them down. (Too bad Jesus wasn't there, He would have kicked the "money-changers" out!! --- Who knows, they may have been getting a kick-back from them -- or maybe it was the Communist's way of allowing them to remain open!)

The visiting Priests must have been irritated by it, for they were really leering at them, indignantly. Even I was offended by it! I couldn't believe anything like that would be tolerated! Flashbulbs were going off like crazy when the Catholicos came down the aisle and sat on His throne. There were a couple of dignitaries who sat near Him, and they looked like they may have come from Beirut.

The Catholicos gave a lengthy Sermon. We lined up in front of the Bema (Altar) for Magart (Host.) Later, I heard a conversation about how exuberant the Catholicos was in His sermonizing, because of the presence of the foreign Armenians. There was a diamond-studded, gold cross on display, for which people, including myself, were lining up to kiss. The denizens and visitors were barbecuing lambs behind the wall, built around the grounds. Had I not been looking for a lavatory, I would never have known there were cooking facilities and tables around, behind the walls. Travelers, from remote places, were feasting all around the spacious grounds. There were a lot of people there; it was a special occasion -- and really, a sight to see! We returned to Yerevan.

My relatives took me to my Aunt "Armenouhi's" daughter's apartment, which they shared.) We ate dinner, and as usual -- more cognac and wine toasts to me. Her twin boys (about 2 years old) put on a show for us. "Ashot" kept turning around until he'd fall over, get up groggily, smiling, and do it over, time and time again.
Later, my cousins, Yura, and Shura-from-Tiflis, caught me a cab and dropped me off at the hotel. My ankles were swollen, and walking was becoming difficult.

September 13th: Monday

I woke up at 8, shaved, dressed and went down to the hotel restaurant at 9:00 A.M. After breakfast, I went, down to the lobby and got my passport to exchange my money. I didn't have time to do so before, because the tours and my relatives kept me too busy. -- Also, my relatives refused to allow it, and got indignant when I previously mentioned it! The bank in the hotel is open from 9:30 A.M. until 3:30 P.M., five days a week. I didn't have to go on tour today, as arrangements were cancelled.

More of my relatives came into town to see me, and from the hotel, we went to Aunt Ovsanna's house. We took more pictures outside, where they stood in front of the cement blocks, which supported the road going up the hill. It seemed humorous, watching all the traffic: going up the hill, with people looking down at us taking pictures -- and yet, it seemed tragic that my aunt had to live here in this environment of dust and fumes. Sometimes the tragedies of life can place a heavy burden on you, and you have to accept the fate of those circumstances. The story one son told me was that, when they were Young, they had an altercation with a man which resulted in a tragic, unpremeditated, mortal finality; getting the two brothers convicted to a lengthy sentence. --And the mother had to give up her life savings, and more, to get them released from a lengthy incarceration. That is about the best thing I have ever heard about Communism-- I wonder how many of those corrupt bastards got rich by controlling other people's lives?! -- Yet, I am not naive enough to think that we freedom loving "Americans" live a life of purity, and don't have corrupt officials! --- But, "yes" -- God did create a perfect world --- and He "didn't" create money! And, with all the hardships my aunt had to endure raising those two boys, whose father had gotten killed in the 2nd World War, and after 25 years of saving money picking grapes for a living - and losing it - she looked a generation older than she was. -- And the boys cherished their mother like a precious diamond, trying to compensate for those years of heartache she endured.

Cousin "Edvard" (my mother's sister, Mariam's son -- from Shahoumian, Verastan "Georgia") played his accordion and we sang-- we ate and drank some more. By this time, my ankles are swollen, and hurt, more. They bathed my feet again. (It was really embarrassing---- them, washing my feet. They wouldn't let me do it! The attention that they heaped on me really made me feel humble. And it's not that I'm not a humble person -- but, "my God" - I'm not "Jesus," that You want to wash my feet! Maybe now you can see how overwhelmed a person can get, having all these emotions being stirred up in You in a compressed time frame!) We came back -to the hotel at 11:00 P.M.

September 14th:

Ate breakfast in the hotel dining room, and then went down to the lobby. Again, my relatives came over -- and brought more, "new" relatives, for me to meet.

I couldn't go on the bus tour with the other tourists because, my ankles were feeling worse; so I went to Aunt Ovsanna's house and spent the day there, taking more pictures. (As Much as it hurt my ankles, I disregarded the pain to take more pictures. Not only for my mother and family to see their relatives, but also to send pictures back to my relatives, after I got home. For it seemed, the only ones there with cameras were the tourists. And -- if any of them wanted to have a picture taken, they had to hire a photographer. --- Maybe the Communists didn't allow them to have any -- I never asked.)

After dinner, they dropped me off at the hotel at 7:30 P.M. -- they wanted me to go to one of the biggest "football" (soccer) games of the year. They had bought tickets a few days before - including mine. I didn't want to spoil their fun, but my ankles were very sore and swollen -- I couldn't concentrate, let alone, walk! -- I wanted to see their newly built stadium, too --- it holds 75,000 people.

I soaked my ankles in cold water, and at 8:30 P.M. my mother's three sisters, Armenouhi, Mariam and Ovsanna came over; concerned with my pain.

They called the hotel doctor and he asked questions (no history of ankle swelling) took my pulse, etc. Then he gave me some sulfa pills, and my Uncle Marklen, later got my salve--prescription filled out at the pharmacy. My Aunts left at 10:30 P.M., only after insisting on allowing them to put salve on my ankles and hearing my reassurance that I'd be alright.

September 15th: Wednesday

I woke up today at 7:30 A.M. and took two More sulfa pills, shaved, and Marklen and Aunts Armenouhi and Ovsan came to see me. The desk-clerk; in charge of my floor, came in again, inquiring about my condition and said the skin doctor would stop in before 4:00 P.M. (I guess they must have thought I may have gotten scratched somewhere and got infected?)

Cousins Yura, Edvard and Aramais came in -- the room was full Of relatives, concerned over me. My Aunts had the floor clerk bring my breakfast to the room. Then they left, leaving me to rest -- and said they would be back at 3:00 P.M. I wrote a few more postcards; this was an opportune time, to do so. My feet felt better at about l:30 P.M. (When I had woken up about 4.30 this morning, my pajama top and pillow were soaking wet.)

At 3:45 P.M. the room maid let the busboy in, with my lunch tray. They're killing me with hospitality!! After finishing my lunch, Uncle Marklen and his son Aramais came in. They asked if I had eaten, and said they were going to the restaurant and wanted to know if there was anything I would like. I asked for "lemonada." About 4:45 P.M. my Aunts came back, while Marklen and his son were talking with me. They brought some chicken soup, with about half a chicken in it! --- Ugh!! (Those who know me, know that I am not an avid chicken fan.) I knew I couldn't eat anymore, so I passed out the chicken and just drank the Soup -- just to be polite. Then, about 5:45, a woman doctor came in, and asked some pertinent questions, and felt that it was something in my system, possibly caused by a scratch, or an insect, also compounded by the aggravation of walking on stones and hills. She said that the sulfa dosage that was prescribed was excessive, and cut it in half, and wrote a prescription for some ointment for my ankles. -- She labeled my malady as "Garmeer-kammi" (Red-wind!) I think she was she talking about the Devil ---or, the Russians? I was humored, wondering what the doctors in the "States" would think of this?' Was it a military secret we hadn't heard of?! (Armenian humor!) A little later, another food tray was brought in, and I declined. All they want you to do is eat, eat, eat! (Who said they're inhospitable in the Soviet Union?)

My female relatives asked about the United States, quite extensively. Most of what they had heard about was not fabricated. They were amazed at the methods of birth control the U.S. was encouraging and found my explanations of vasectomy operations, humorous. They said the Soviet government was paying $300.00) for each child that was born. My Aunts left at 11:00 P.M. Cousin Yura, and Edvard and his wife stayed for another hour.-- They asked questions about life in the U.S. relevant to our family, what we had, how many children in each family, etc. After they left, I took another pill and went to sleep.

September 16th; Thursday
I woke up at 3:00 A.M., took another sulfa pill, removed my wet pajama top) and went back to bed. Woke up at 7:30 A.M., shaved and dressed. Yura and Edvard and Jura came over about 8:20. They're going to take me to Ovsan's for the day, to rest my feet -- rather than sit at the hotel all day. I watched the tourists from my balcony, going on their various trips.

We went down to the main floor, and Yura went to speak to the hotel official about my release. --- After a couple of hours, Yura came smiling, toward us, and said: "Let's go!" --- While riding in the cab, he told us he bribed the official and got his permission to take me, and was told: "Do whatever you want." (My Uncle was more naive or, probably more cautious than Yura, and hadn't considered bribery. Some Armenians, if they knew him, may have considered him a "surreega"---a rogue-- but I will say it would be more apropos to call him "Jarr-beeg" --- a fast learner, wiser. I would say he was capable of doing anything he set his mind to, cunning and smart, soft spoken and gentlemanly, yet capable of taking care of himself in any situation, and not intimidated by anyone -- although he was of average size. I liked him, but he was adept at coercion with his relatives, in a non-combative way. I guess you can acquire a lifestyle like that when you're incarcerated and with nefarious characters! Yet -- his older brother was more of a serious, quieter type of guy, and not extroverted like Yura. Maybe it was because he was married, with children, and Yura wasn't. They both did "time" together, and both younger than me. -- My cousins!!)

Later, Cousins Yura and Edvard went to Erebuni, upon the request of Yura's mother, to get some "special" dirt from the site, for my sore ankles. My Aunts mixed some "madzoon" (yogurt) and put it on my ankles to cool them; and later, when my cousins came back with the dirt, the women mixed it with vinegar, made a mud-pack out of it and covered my ankles with it! (Before they mixed it though, Aunt Ovsan was outside, squatting down near the ground, and sifting the dirt with a screen. It seemed as though their only concern in life was to tend to me, as if I was a king. -- It was a feeling difficult to express -- unless it happened to you. I felt so humble. -- My Dear Aunts. -- Aunts that I didn't know before -- And loving me like "this" -- a total stranger!!)\

But, before they put the mud pack on, they went through an old Armenian (?) ritual of blessing my feet, by using a gold-looking

coin, rubbing it in circles around my ankles, and saying words and uttering "thoo-thoo" -- as if spitting at the disease in my feet. About an hour later, they washed and dried my feet, and still they felt they couldn't do enough! I wanted to wash my own feet but they, insisted! (It was humiliating to me, the amount of love and attention they heaped on me. - And my wondering, if we in America, would have responded toward them in a similar manner if the situation had been reversed!) Later, Shura (with the blue eyes; my mother's oldest brother's son) and Marklen, came back from touring the town, in Yerevan -- they're both out-of-towners -- and they must have had a few drinks. (Note: Shura's mother had lost her 30-year-old married daughter two years ago, but my Aunts never, wrote to my mother about it for fear it may have been bad for her heart.) The daughter died because she refused to allow the doctors permission to cut off her cancerous leg -- and the cancer spread throughout her body. They also made mention of a girl ((second cousin)) that was killed by an auto while she was running to get a doctor for a
relative.) Half an hour later, while Uncle Marklen was asleep, Shura started to play games with his own son, Ashot (aged two?) They were throwing and spitting water at each other and having fun, while also fighting with him with a plastic pole and he accidentally deflected the pole onto his wife's nose! Well, his wife's nose began bleeding, and she didn't even get angry! What, loving people. While her nose was bleeding (nobody got excited -- as if it was nothing,) and she was washing off the blood in the sink, her- husband threw water on the back of her neck, as if helping, but more so, as if trying to anger her and deliberately soaking her hair. It was a sink on the outside of the house, newly installed, for a bathroom Ovsan's sons were building. Here she was, trying to stop the nose-bleed, in the sink, and at the same time laughing and fighting off her husband -- while from the other side, her son Ashot was still trying to hit his father, although he was hitting his mother at times, too! His father just kept splashing and spitting water- at his son! --- It really was something, lasted about 20 minutes, and everybody was laughing! (Would an

"American" wife have reacted that way?! -- Hell no! Maybe that's why we have so many ulcer cases in the U.S.!) In the evening, a relative of Shura's came over. Their wives are sisters. Later, about six of us, men, went for a ride up to the top of Yerevan -- to the "aigee" (really called, "Haghtanagee aiguh" -- which means "Victory Gardens,") and walked around, there. It was night-time, and the lights in the city were glowing, and you could see for over a mile into the distance. It was the most beautiful sight of a city that I've ever seen at night. They showed me the statue of "Myrr Haiastan" (Mother Armenia) that was quite tall (200 feet?) and quite impressive -- for she held a large sword in her hands, in readiness to protect her "Armenian" children! -- It was also on top of the enormous hill overlooking the city. You can't lose your direction in Yerevan - no matter where you go, you'll always see her! At the base of the statue there was a plaque with a wreath, with an inscription to the memory of all those who died during the genocide. We sat at some tables there on the hill, at a refreshment stand, and listened to an orchestra playing Music.

Later we went to our relative's apartment and they showed us their new piano, which they had recently purchased. We had some champagne, and again, they toasted me for my honor and presence. Later, we went back to Ovsanna's house (Edvard was playing the accordion) and Aunt Armenouhi danced, a couple of my cousins sang. They really sang some emotionally, sad songs. About 10:45 P.M. Shura and his and Edvard and his family had to go back toward Tiflis. We went to the train station to see them off. They had a large loaf of bread, some cheese, and a bottle of cognac (wrapped up.) The bottle-top must have been loose, for the Conductor sensing the smell knew what it was -- and he asked what they had, "wrapped up?" and they said, "Bread!" And he said: "Ayio, geedem hots eh!" ("Yeah, I know it's 'bread!'") -- while he twisted-up his nose and rolled his eyes! I guess you're not supposed to drink on the train, as some of the relatives seemed apprehensive, as if disciplinary action would be taken. It was a fairly good-sized train-station, for being in the middle of nowhere; but, I'm certain the natives must really appreciate it, for their lack of private automobiles. The Davit of Sassoon statue stands out, in front of the station, probably as a reminder of days gone by! (If you know of any Armenians that know about the statue, ask them to tell you the story about his sword!)

I slept overnight at Aunt Ovsanna's home. It was the first night that I slept without having some inebriate yelling in the middle of the night. (As I heard every night, when the late party-goers would leave the Hotel cafe) - yet, my aunt's house is only 50 feet from the side of the road that goes up the mountain, with intermittent vehicle movement all night. But the irony of it was that I was sleeping at the front of the house, like on a front porch, for it was supposed to be an additional room, but the windows had not been installed yet. Cousin Yura said that was his bed he relinquished to me, with a sense of pride, in my honor --and it was wooden construction with a mattress on it. I didn't want to inconvenience him, but he insisted. And since I wanted to have an experience of living the everyday Armenian life, I stayed. And one thing which I appreciated was that I don't recall ever having a mosquito bite me --- probably because of the rocky-surfaced area, or lack of stagnant pools of water, because it was summer, and hot.

September 17th: Friday
I woke up at 7:30 A.M. to a nice, cool morning. It was the first time in a week that I had slept more than 6 hours in a night. Maybe it was because it was too warm in the hotel, since they didn't have air-conditioning -- or even a fan! (For a new hotel, you would think they would have considered it.) I mean, for this time of the year, the temperatures were running from 85' to over 100' F. during the day! As I laid there on the bunk, of the newly constructed front room, I watched the cars, buses and pedestrians going by, and I don't know what was more of a sight ---"me" -- or them! Kids with red neckerchiefs, going to town --- workers, going to work. 'They do a considerable amount of walking for city folks. The buses don't move until they are jammed to the point of people hanging

out of the doors. It's surprising that the patrons still pay their fare, even with an established law to fine non-payers, after hanging-outside of the bus. The system is corrupt to a point of permissiveness, for the government knows that the driver is making a little extra money by over-capacity of fares. They say it's attributable to a lack of buses, but I think it's an excuse to subjugate the Armenians and their morale! ---- Arid they say everything is free in the Soviet Union!! After breakfast, we talked for a while, and later we went to the hotel so I could shave. We looked at prices in a few stores; they have fairly well material in clothing -- however, their prices are two or three times higher-- than ours in the United States. They have all the necessities in apparel, but are lacking in fineries, and frivolities. Socks and undershirts were lower than our prices. Hardware was two to three times lower than ours, but couldn't compare in quality, or variety.

First to note; is the "Housing" condition---- Who, would buy tools when the government owns the apartment houses and keeps up (supposedly) repairs? Why would anyone, who isn't overly ambitious, (or a Party member) want to keep his ramshackle house repaired, when the government has given him notification of tearing down his home and compulsorily moving him into an apartment-house?! Secondly--- how can anyone afford to live, and buy clothing, when the average worker earns a dollar an hour and only works 35 hours per week? (7 hours a day, 5 days a week is their-normal workweek.)

The jewelry and watches were half the price of ours. The price of, shoes were comparable to prices of our best shoe stores, ranging from $15.00 to $50.00. The only difference is that in Armenia you can buy them ready-made, or have them made for the same price. The department stores are large enough, but very under-supplied! It seemed like I had gone back to my childhood days, while walking through the 5-and-10 cent stores. -- They were like stores we had 35 years ago. There were no elevators or escalators, and their stairs were made from marbled tiles, with

wooden, creaky floors. The service was slow, and the clerks seemed to work with typical monotony and rarely smiled. It seemed everyone in charge of the public felt they were better or smarter than the poor folks that were shopping. There were a few women that were looking at a knit dress-suit that had just arrived from France, with a price tag of $80.00 (Rubles
were slightly higher than our US dollar) and there was no doubt in my mind that a few of them planned on purchasing it! That sort of made me wonder about their system and everyone being equal!' --- There were people walking around the outskirts of town, in clothing that reflected "destitution" ---- yet, in the center of town, most of them dressed as well as our city folk, or better.

The amount of white shirts worn by the men becomes monotonous after awhile, and it reminded me of old man Henry Ford who, when speaking of his Model "A" cars, would say: "Give them any color they want -- as long as it's black."

We went to the pharmacy and had to go through the same routine as we did in the stores. We first had to stand in line to see what we wanted, and then go to another line to pay, and come back to the purchase line with the purchase-slip to get the item. It seemed the government wasn't too concerned about doing anything about the excessive and unnecessary delay. (That's another way of keeping everyone employed.) --- And yet, in retrospect, it seemed a more foolproof system of having any employee trying to cheat the system. For, now, you could have three people going to Siberia, if caught!!

On the fringe of town, the poor women have to walk up and down hills, over stones, through dust, take buses and carry large bags of groceries. -- And I rarely saw men-folk display courtesy, or chivalry toward them --- even as much as standing up to allow them to sit on a bus, or stepping aside when approaching them on the sidewalks! The men are all chauvinistic. The women carry a big load here, and they don't even complain. (The American housewife would never make it here! Must be a form of Women's Liberation in the USSR-- caused by a shortage of men killed during the war. 25,000,000 ?)

After Supper, my Uncle's wife "Tamara" came back from Kirovagan, and we went for a ride into town, and sat by the water-fountain in the park and talked with Cousin Yura, and Aramais. We returned after dark, had tea with my 3 aunts (my mother's sisters) and talked some more about life in the USA The women were still chatting when I went to bed at 12:30 A.M.

September 18th: Saturday
I woke up at 7:30 A.M. After we had breakfast, my aunts were still fussing over my sore ankles. Later, 12:00 P.M., we went to the "Zoo." It was near the top of the hill, in town. Everything has to be done by cab or bus, here; it's too difficult to do otherwise. You walk for miles, and most of it is up and down hills. You can spend hours waiting for buses, and then they crowd you in before they move. The extra passengers must be the driver's bonus -- and according to my cousin, it must be true! -- "This" is the glorious USSR!! The powerful regime that made the world quake in fear. The regime that abused its working class, and built a Military Empire off of the sweat of its people -- with modern military warfare, yet, compelling its masses to work like jackasses with antiquated turn-of-the-century machinery. When I saw farmers pulling sleds (I mean, no "wheels") on the farms -- I couldn't believe it!! I knew then, that it was a matter of time before it would crumble! --I, at least, felt the Chinese would outlast the Russians -- for it was the Chinese who were criticizing the Russians for having a corrupt "Communist" system!! But, history has shown that no nation will last without allowing its masses to vent their frustration. The U.S. is the modern example of that hypothesis; -- let everyone scream, and tomorrow they won't even remember what they were yelling about!! We spent the day at Ovsanna's. When she would see us get off of the bus by her house, she'd always come to greet me and hold my hand -- as if I was made of

gold or, something precious. She was only five years older than I, but looked like she was sixty. Poor Ovsan, she worked so hard --- and never once, complained. Nevertheless, at times she'd remind me of a girl of 20; she seemed to be so pure of heart, and lighthearted -- so altruistic and innocent. Yet, she was so wise, and had endured so much --being left a widow at a young age, with two boys to raise. I imagine many Armenian women fell into that category. My four, other Aunts that I saw, were widowed, also caused from the Second World War.

September 19th: Sunday
I woke up) at 7:30 A.M. and the women were already up and about. It seemed every time I washed up someone was there, handing me a towel before I could reach for it. We had a late breakfast, and about 11:00, Tamara came in and greeted me with a bouquet of flowers. Cousin Yura got into an argument with her, later. It turned out that she wanted to take me to Kirovagan, but cousin Yura refused her my company. -- I didn't want anyone deciding for me, but at the same time, being unfamiliar with their customs, I didn't want to seem rude let alone, inhospitable, by criticizing Yura for bossing her like that. I sensed though that the men in Armenia are more authoritative and have the final word. Tamara cried -- and I felt bad -- and later, Yura explained that when her husband (Marklen) arrived the next day, "he" would make that decision -- and not her! (Armenian chauvinism?)

My paternal cousin (2nd cousin) Davit came over around noon, and we hugged each other, and he asked Aunt Ovsanna if she'd mind if he took me to Keghart. She left it up to me, saying it was all right with her. Davit had a friend of his, who owned a cab, drive us there. His wife, Svetanna, and their child, daughter went also. We stopped on the road, near a small town, and Davit bought some apples. The villagers looked at us in awe. It seemed if you were dressed up, you must be someone important! They were dressed like the peasants, in movies.

My cousin Davit, of all the relatives I met, not only reflected the attitude of a man with authority, but possessed it, also. He was a hydroelectric engineer and must have had more voice than an average person, or even a schoolteacher. You must belong to the "Party" or you don't get any higher than a laborer, it seems! Although, he was very mannerly and cultured, and above all, I noticed he spoke respectfully to the peasants, even though it was with an air of authority and dignity. It took us over an hour to get to Keghart. As we approached the area, you could feel the excitement in the air. There were cars and buses parked all over the place. It was really bustling with people.

The ancient church was built in 1283 AD, and was carved out of solid rock, inside and out. It's unbelievable what the Armenians had done, considering the era and the primitive tools that they must have had at that time. The main ceiling must have been over 50 high, and there were separate chambers -- the largest section being over 2,500 square feet of floor space. The ceiling was supported-by stone-columns, also, carved out of the same, solid-rock mountain. The ceiling was domed. There were other small rooms with coves, fitted with statues. It seemed the floor had trough-like impressions carved out for water to flow through; possibly a drainage system for the water that seeped into the building. --- Or, who knows -- possibly for a hot water heating system? If I remember correctly, the church was built out of solid rock to fend off invaders, with more protection, and less damage to the structure. The walls on the inside were black, possibly from the soot, of fires built for lighting and heat. There was a steady flow of visitors passing through this ancient treasure, left to us for our heritage from the legacy of our dedicated Christian artisans. On the outside surrounding grounds, I observed the natives in awe, bringing butchered chickens, and even live lambs to the Monastery, as gift offerings, and some to be blessed for their own consumption -- and they were butchering them right out in front, by the surrounding wall. The front of the Monastery had a stone wall about 15 feet high, protecting it from the only road accessible to it, for the two sides were flanked by mountain walls and the back side rose into another one. It seemed impregnable, except from the front!

The natives were wining and dining all around the hillside, and music could be heard echoing around the mountains with the sounds of merry-making. There is an axiom about not missing something until you don't have it anymore -- but in my case, it was just the opposite! It was something I realized I missed, because I never had it before! This could have been "my country" to have been born in if it had not been for the damned, fiendish Turks. -- And then, right there in that glorious mountain setting, I thought about my friend Carl Saroukhanian, who would always and instinctively say: "shoonerruh!" ("The dogs!") when- ever someone mentioned the word "Turk." -- Come to think of it, my mother-in-law, who was orphaned from the Genocide used to endear the Turks with that same phrase -- and I say "endear" because that was one of her more polite words for "them!"

And now, I suppose someone may wonder how some "Christians" can think like that! And my answer to that would be: If you lost your family, or half of your "Christian Armenian" population, or your roots to your ancestral lands -- and the "Christian" countries who pretended they were going to help you in those perilous days, departed, leaving you to suffer the additional atrocities and years later become allies to the same country that perpetrated those heathen acts -- how much "Christian" feelings can you imagine would be left in your Soul?! ---- Yes - I tried to extend those "Christian" beliefs to them --- but I can't stop the sun from shining! But the Turks did! At least for the 1,547,231 "Christian" Armenians they exterminated! But, "Judgement Day" will come! And that's what keeps most Armenians from terrorist-acts of vengeance. For we don't only believe, in the "Old Testament," like some of the non-Christian countries, we live by the New Testament.

After we left Keghart, Davit suggested we stop at a nearby diner. He ordered a large tray of lamb, bread, lemonada, cheese, and I can't remember what else -- but it was too much. Wow! It was delicious!

You can't possibly imagine the enormity of the hills until you look at them for awhile; they're awesome! We were surrounded by, them! I'm certain the Empire State Building would have looked dwarfed by them. Everything seemed to be of solid rock, with trees and grass on it. Davit's friend bought me a cross for a souvenir. By the time we got back to Yerevan, and Ovsanna's house, she had supper cooked -- eggplant and tomatoes, peppers and "khorrovads"("roast lamb", in big chunks with bones on them.) The fire was made of wood, on the stone ground out in front, and the vegetables were whole. -- What big skewers-- about 3 feet long! "Reuben" (who was a shoemaker at the state-operated shoe-factory) is the son of my mother's father's brother.)??!! (Since I never had any relatives in the U.S.A. I had to describe him like that! .--- Would you believe that. --- I didn't know he was my "Great Uncle" until I got home and figured it Out!! I thought he was a cousin! There were so many relatives coming and going that it made my head swim. I was stupefied!!) --And Reuben's mother "Astkhig," came with him -- and she is, "Anitchkha's" sister! --- Anitchkha -- I used to hear her name all the time when our mother used to tell us stories about her youth, and what they used to do back home, in Shahumian, Georgia, USSR. We took some more pictures outside -- I just had to have them to show my mother -- that was even more important to me than my own mementos -- to bring back some of her dreams that she had left behind; since, she was the eldest in her family. My dear mother - how I wished she had been there with me! Kevork "Jora" (Yura's younger brother) had bought a lamb the day before, for my birthday on the 23rd, and we had some laughs about the lamb becoming a sacrifice for me. It was really a ram, with curled horns, and they came walking it home with them, tied onto a rope! These relatives are really something else! They don't have much, but they do their utmost to give you the royal treatment! They say: That's all there is in life --- eat and drink good. Later that evening, Yura and I went to the Ani Hotel, to my room, and took a shower. We talked for a while with a Mrs. Serabian (from Detroit area -- Lincoln Park) and later, with another woman (Helen, German) who made the same trip. They said they missed me (since I was staying at my Aunt's) and said they were sorry to hear about my sore ankles. We went back to Ovsan's about 11:30 P.M., and talked until 1:00 A.M. -- while looking at some old pictures they had save, in a wooden chest.

September 20th: 1971 Monday
I woke up at 7:30 A.M. to the clattering of women's shoe-heels, and saw Tamara and Uncle Marklen walking around. When they saw that I was awake, Tamara came toward me with a big smile on her face, and kissed me. She was glad to be back, and with her husband, knowing that now he would be able to make the "man's decision" to take me to Kirovagan (his home town.) We left Yerevan at 3:45 A.M., after first finagling a deal with an illicit cab driver. (There was a whole street-full of private cars being used as cabs -- so I don't know what kind of a deal or joke that was with the government.) We got to the village of Dilijan -- the roads were out of this world -- winding, twisting, bumpy, up-and-down slopes ---- but the view of the countryside is really breathtaking, and an artist would really rave at the sights rarely seen by people from the outside world. The different types of faces, long-beards, villagers sitting at the roadside -- ancient homes! The homes all seemed to favor the same colors: red, white, and blue -- predominantly, blue. We stopped at a roadside store (perhaps a village grocery,) which was on the main road (two lane highway,) to buy something to eat. There were about 4 women and a man employed there. We bought some lunch-meat, bread and lemonada. Driving down the road about 2 miles, we found a scenic, roadside place, where we could eat. There was a running stream down below. Someone had built a gazebo with a monument erected next to it, in memory of a loved one, named

"Ofeeg." --- As I wondered about the love for Ofeeg, I couldn't help but wonder how long a gazebo like this would last in the U.S.A. We got to Kirovagan about noon. The main part of town had a fairly large Square (as did most cities that I saw in Armenia.) It seemed to be more of an industrial city, and didn't seem to have the atmosphere of congeniality, as Yerevan did. The people seemed to live a much drabber life there. Like everything looked grey. A railroad ran through the town, and there was a large factory spewing yellow smoke out of its chimney, which seemed, from sulpher! -- And when I asked my Uncle what they made there, he said he didn't know, and he has lived there long enough   --- and neither did anyone else!!! We walked around town, and I noticed a bus depot there and couldn't help but feel that the travel of the citizens was quite controlled by the Soviets, because the police were omnipresent there (probably for checking passports!) The cab drivers seemed to have it made in Armenia (like they have their own union) and are their own bosses. We took a cab to Uncle Marklen's apartment.

The apartment complexes here are older and in near disrepair. They are drab looking. I noticed a well-pump at the outside of the building -- and later understood, "why?." They shut the water supply off when there's a need to make repairs in an apartment, and when this happens --- "Oh, Boy!" Their services are terrible in the USSR. Nobody hurries to make repairs! The day that I was there, the water was turned off and was still off the next day! Why should people attempt to repair anything, when the government owns everything?--So, nobody cares!! My Uncle lived on the 4th floor; the stairways weren't too well illuminated, and were made of cement and steel. It was in fair shape. His apartment had a small bathroom with a hot water heater in it, a kitchen, a living room and dining room combined, and one bedroom. Fortunately they lived on the corner of the building, and had a nice cross-breeze. All, the windows had ledges, and most of the people had flowerpots on them. Across the street, about half a mile away, was a large rolling hill about 500 feet high, with a forest that adjoined the distant mountains, and Aunt Tamara said that in the summer, when it was hot, they would go picnicking there. A lady friend of theirs drove us around town in her "maakena" "machine" (car) and we came to where a crowd of about 200 people had gathered, and they were watching a young teenaged girl walk a tightrope (with a long pole in her hands, and bottles stacked on her head) while a "doodoog" or "zoorna" (a wooden flute, or clarinet?) and a drum accompanied her with "noise"--- and in the crowd milled a clown (about age 60) who was ridiculing the people in a jesting way about their parsimony (stinginess) and collecting donations. -- It was really a sight to see the townspeople gawking at her, but it was more of a thrill, for me, to see the expressions on their faces. A nostalgic feeling overcame me during the course of reflection (my father's country)--- and I wondered if I could have been one of the gawkers if I had been born there, instead of in the "United States of America." ---I couldn't help but feel sorry for them, their deprivation, uneducated, simple people, uncomplicated, and uncorrupted minds, and I somehow wished I was born there, too -- as I fought hard to keep the tears from flowing. It was really, a hell-of-a mixed-up, emotional feeling' -- To think they were looking at me as if I was somebody (since it wasn't difficult to spot a foreigner -- mod shoes and blue shirt -- updated clothes are hard to come by, here.) --- I felt like yelling: "I'm no better than You!" -- I felt so pretentious receiving all that attention. The population of Kirovagan is 250,000. We returned to the apartment and had dinner. Tamara took such pride in cooking her meal -- she wanted to show me how capable she was. -- It was really an elaborate meal. -- What a variety! She, was-all smiles! We had more cognac, and a few neighbors came over and we talked for a couple of hours. Marklen excused himself and went out to see about transportation to Tiflis, Georgia. He returned about an hour later, with a smile on his face. He had hired a cab for tomorrow (it must have cost him $40.00 for the whole day.) We planned on leaving before 6:30 A.M.-- It was now 11:45 P.M. -- and Marklen (who is a barber, in town) gave his son Aramais a haircut. (His barbershop is a 6-foot square wooden-box, painted canary-yellow, and situated on the sidewalk, at a large corner, off the edge of town.) Tamara brought me a large pail of warm water to soak my feet, and when I finished, cousin Yura insisted that he'd soak his feet in the same water. (The women are really subservient to the men--folk, here.) It was near midnight, and we, cousin Yura and I, were offered the twin--beds of my Aunt and Uncle. I never saw such large pillows in all my life --- and the mattresses really, sagged. It was really a funny thing -- cousin Yura and I looked at each other and laughed. It felt like.I was sitting up when I laid down!

We woke up at 5:50 A.M., left Kirovagan at 6:35 -- and arrived at Alahverdi an hour later. Aunt Armenouhi and some of my relatives live here, also. The mountain roads are hell to drive on; especially on the automobile. The driving time from Kirovagan to Tiflis is three hours, and it's 108 miles (180 kilometers x .6 = 108 miles. -- To be exact, it's really .621.) We drove to Shoulaver, Verastan-(Georgia) and got there at I:00 A.M. The cabbie had "problems" with his car and he really went through some act pretending he was really doing something difficult (to reflect on his importance) --- actually, he was partially ignorant of what he was doing, though he thought he knew. (I had majored in auto mechanics in school, but I refrained from interceding, just to see what he knew -- and to see if he was trying to rip-off my Uncle. If this book is ever read in Armenia ("Rip-off" in America, means, when someone is trying to take advantage of you, monetarily.) In the Soviet Union, you don't get a driver's license unless you know the basic mechanical parts of an automobile, in order to make your own repairs if you're stranded on the road. -- Garages are few and far in-between towns! -- And that's understandable, but, I presume it was another tactic of controlling who got licenses, and more payoffs.) When we reached Shoulaver (Shou-la-verr,) my mother's birthplace, we hadn't gone 200 yards onto a side street (road) when we got a flat tire. The road was really terrible; like it was paved with jagged rocks!' We were near a school there, and it seemed all the school children gathered around to see what was going on. Uncle Marklen chased them away, while the flat tire was being fixed by the "cabbie"(cabdriver.) Tamara, my Uncle and I walked up the street to the edge of town, toward the cemetery, to see my grandparents' graves. The sight I saw amazed and saddened me. At the foot of the hill (200 feet high) there were gravestones that were toppled over, and it seemed as if it may have been where the cemetery originated, and may have been over a hundred years old. They were totally neglected. I questioned my Uncle of their neglect, and he said: "El marrt chee mnahtseh orr hok danneh." (Note to non-Armenians-- all A's are pronounced as the A in "ah".) "There's nobody else left to take care of it.") As we walked up the hill, I noticed that the graves improved in appearance, considering they were newer graves. The newer graves had wrought iron fences around them. My Grandparents' (Marklen's parents) lot had an 8 foot square fence around it. As I stood there, thinking about the first-and only- letter that I had written to my Grandmother (83, whom, it seemed, had waited decades to receive a letter from me before passing away), I couldn't help but feel that I had contributed to her death. -- For, had I not written to her, she may have tenaciously held-on to her dreams of her daughter's (my mother) outcome in life. Now her saddened heart had been laid to rest, after my divulgence to her of her daughter "Varsenik's" tribulations and transpirations in life in the "foreign country" of the "United States of America."

(Note! Some of "Varsenik's" tribulations, written in the preface of this book --"The Apkarians.") With this thought in mind, coupled with the fact that I had never seen my Grandparents that I had always yearned to see, I broke down and started to cry. It seemed my emotions had a chain reaction -- for my Aunt and Uncle began crying, also. The other thoughts adding to my lachrymose state were: "It seemed as if I had waited all my life to come to this village, to this very spot, and felt as if I was being born again -- for some reason." In those ethereal moments of sorrow, I realized I could have been born here, instead of the U.S.A., if my parents hadn't moved. In that moment, I had the greatest urge to scream out: "You Turkish bastard, Talaat, may you burn in hell for all the turmoil and deaths you caused my Armenian people!" (God forgive me, for saying that --and that's more than what any Turk ever said -- for they never asked for "forgiveness!") --- With my mixed emotions, it made me realize I could have been an ignorant kid, living in a village that seemed as if time had stood still since the birth of Armenia. (Although this was an Armenian village in Georgia -- my father was born in Shirak -- which is across the border from Leninakan -- Not in "Turkish" Armenia -- but --- in Turkish held "Armenian" territory! To "me" - it will never be "Turkish" Armenia! It also made me realize how fortunate I was, knowing I had had a better education and a life that any villager here could never have dreamt of beyond his wildest imagination.

The main street leading into the village was about three car lanes wide, unpaved, and with sidewalks at certain points. My mother's home (birthplace) was right off of the main street-(10 feet wide), and it was a few feet below street level (and at the lower level of town --closer to the vineyards.) It had an attic on top, maybe 30 feet long, and the front porch was facing East -- into the direction of the main road coming into town -- and it had 7 brown, wooden posts on it.

I tried to envision the stories our mother used to tell us about, like when her father used to come riding into town in the wintertime on his horse and sleigh. He used to be a merchant. It could easily be a mile from the highway and the railroad that passes by,. It must have been something, half-a-century ago, to have had a home like she had, for I didn't see too many homes like it during my travel there. The streets were all hard dirt, and the side streets were really bad -- large, sharp and bumpy stones. You'd think they'd be in better condition, for the amount of cars that they had there, were a rarity. If I was to have estimated the population of the village, I would have said 1,000 people; however, factually, I heard there were 10,000. My mother told me, during her youth the whole town had flooded away by the waters coming from the fissures in the mountains. After seeing the town from atop the hill of the cemetery, it can be easily, believed that the population was so large. The scenic view really displayed the enormity of the valley! I saw a church, named St Sarkis, at the top of the hill, and I would guess it could easily be 500 feet above the lower part of town. My Uncle Marklen showed me the 7 rock boulders at the top of the hill, across from the cemetery. On the other side of the village, across the valley, there was another landmark boulder with a hole in it -- and that's why they call it "dzog-karr"= (hole-rock.) We drove through the village and met a couple of the relatives (who had visited me in Yerevan) and they were told, in whispered words, that they shouldn't spread the word about my presence until I had left town -- because I hadn't received permission to leave Yerevan. Uncle Marklen and Tamara wanted to take me to see their "aigee" (vineyard,) but I graciously declined, realizing that we didn't have much time, and that they were being nice to me. We drove to Shura's house (my cousin with one arm) and they made dinner for us and insisted we stay. They wouldn't have had it any other way. They acted as if they just couldn't do enough for us. The house was a two-story building, and possibly 50 years old. They had an outdoor toilet attached to the house -- on the front porch of, the second floor! I kept mentioning the name of "Aneetchkha" (my mother's cousin-- and the often-mentioned name from her childhood memories.) But, they probably felt that others in town would have felt slighted if one saw me, and the others didn't. I didn't want to impose on them, so I didn't insist.

Before we left Shoulaver, Shahoumian, Georgia, my cousin Shura wanted - and insisted that he buy some gifts for my three girls, and took us into a small store (where the street divides) and asked me to pick out anything that they might like. I told him that they had everything they wanted, and picked out some inexpensive, costume jewelry -- necklaces. The village was much more like rolling plains, rather than large hills like, everywhere else we had been. As we parted, I wondered if we would ever see each other again -- the thought sort of left me with an empty feeling.

Alahverdi, was the next town we came to as, we headed toward Tiflis. There were large structures built into the sides of the mountain, which looked as if they were constructed for storage places, to shelter goods. And a railroad track passed underneath the mountain, as if a place to seclude the train, and then I found out it was built by the British, during the Second World War. It seemed indestructible and actually did supply and shelter goods for the troops! At another point, where we passed over a small river, there seemed to be a construction which, looked like a conveyor system from the mountain down to the water, where it seemed there may have been a system of loading and unloading small boats, or barges. As we came into Alahverdi, it seemed as if the town was built in the center of a volcano, with houses running up the sides of the mountain. It seemed like the end of the world -- like something out of a Jules Verne novel! The name of the town really does justice to its title-- "Alah" meaning "God" in Arabic (who at one time controlled some parts of that world) and "Verdi" (in Spanish: "garden" = whom the Arabs also controlled once). Or- it may be a combination of Arabic, and Armenian for the Verdi, but with a dialectical mispronunciation for "vardi" or really should be "vardeer"= which means "put down"; where "Verdi" means "put up"= connoting, "God Put it down" -- but I'm inclined to think it's Arabic/Spanish "God's/Garden." But, over the centuries, it's easily understandable how it may have been contorted. From what I've experienced, the emigrated-Armenians have probably retained their language more tenaciously than those in Armenia -- for it seems they may have "slanged" it, somewhat comparable to the way the Americans have slanged the "English" language -- or to put it more correctly, butchered the hell out of it!   Well, what the hell does a retired steelworker know about language, anyway?! But, give me a 4-Hi cold--rolled reversing mill and I'll show You a language about steel -- from .280 hog-iron, to 1008 rim, to .010 high carbon with a variation of plus or minus .0005! -- and, to give you an idea of that last number -- it's like taking an average human hair of about .003

thick, and slicing it lengthwise into 6 pieces, and just take one of those pieces! That's like taking a razor blade (.010) and keeping it in tolerance of one piece of that hair!! (Now you can see why some dummy believed in giving us Steelworkers a 13 week paid vacation once every five years. ---- And put half of them out of work!!)

    Okay --- I'm sorry I got carried away, but I didn't want you to fall asleep. Just checking! Let's get back to the story! ------

    One example of "language," was when my Uncle Mar-klen said: "Gotseenk?" -- when he was asking me if we should go -- when he should have said: "errtank?" --for what he really said was: "we left?" And when I questioned him about this --- he said: "Well, that's the way we've accustomed ourselves to say it." --- and just shrugged his shoulders.

    If anyone can possibly make the trip to AlahvL-rdi, I'd say it's practically a must for anyone going to Armenia. It's beyond words to really describe it with justice. We drove to Tiflis, Georgia, from Alaverdi and the trip took another hour.

    Tiflis is really a large and exceptionally, modern city. Its population is 1,750,000). You can get to it by all means of travel. It is really a, sprawling metropolis! The city is modern and very old -- depending on which part of the city you're in. We drove all over town before concluding it was futile trying to find a place where we could get a drink, wash up, or even "go!" There wasn't one gas station to be seen all the while we drove from one end of town to the other! We stopped in the middle of town -- on a side street --- and walked into a board--walled, enclosed courtyard of a private residence (where people lived in small two-flat homes) and finally found a place to wash up in the center of the courtyard. There was a pipeline over a deep well - probably used by at least five families, and an outdoor toilet - with no running water. We walked around town and then took a subway to the outer perimeter, near its diameter. The escalator was about 450 feet long, and on a decline of about 40 degrees, and traveled about two feet per second -- which was quite rapid for an escalator. It cost only five cents for the subway - and you can travel from one

end of town to the other. It was better illuminated than any other subway I've been on, including New York, London, or Moscow! The seats were covered with leather (New York's is straw, and London's was best, with cloth, but you paid more for the velvet seats if you were dressed up, or you'd wait for the other less expensive train with working--man's straw seats. We took an overhead, suspended, cable car to get to the top part of town. It was about 40 feet above the ground, at its highest point. They had another system, also, which had tracks on the ground, operated with wheels and gears. The hill was quite steep, though --- we may have gone up about 600 feet. When we got to the top, there was a park to walk around in, with flower gardens, confectionery stands, and a small amusement park. There were benches all around, where you could sit and observe the beauty of the city, below. There was an enormous restaurant there, with large stone pillars (about 35 feet high) all around the outer walls of the building, supporting an overhanging roof, for those who desired to dine outside. My uncle Marklen spared no expense on the dinner for me, and my two Cousins; (one from Tiflis, that we picked up, and his wife) and Aunt Tamara, and the Cabbie. The table was really covered with food -- and, you guessed it -- more "cognac'" The waiters were as professional as any waiters I'd seen -- courteous, and attentive. Uncle Marklen left a good tip, too. He gave Tamara some money to buy some gifts for me to bring home, and she couldn't travel fast enough to see if there was anything else that might please me! -- She just wouldn't take "no" for an answer! (She reminded me so much of my wife, in a way, only, 12 years younger.) Later, we went to cousin Jureeg's house (who lives in Tiflis) and washed up and shaved, and had more to eat and drink, before we departed. I couldn't help but notice, while we were washing-up at their well in the courtyard, how large the rats were that were running around, next to one of the other homes. - I mean, bigger than cats!! The neighborhood was quite old. --- It made me wonder about the way of life - --------
--

Cousin Jureeg turned his TV on to show me his affluence; poor guy -- what values mankind places on status symbols -- and there were "only," 2 stations! One channel had a movie, and the other had some government politicians in a discussion. The living conditions that I saw in all my travels, there, were comparable to our standards of about 25 to 50 years ago. We bid them farewell about 8:00 P.M., and there were tears in my Aunt's eyes (my Aunt through marriage, to one of my mother's brothers --- missing in action, during W.W.2.) She was really glad to see someone related to them, coming back to the old country to see relatives. --- I know I really shouldn't say "coming back," or the "old country" -- since I had never been there before -- but, in spirit, that's how nostalgic I felt because of my mother's stories. ----It sort of reminds me of an Irish song I used to sing, when I would play my guitar --- that said. "How can you call it the 'old country' when it will always be Young in my heart." And that would always remind me of Armenia, and bring tears to my eyes! -- Ah -- the Irish." I wondered how much more they would have fought if they didn't have "Christians" for enemies, but Turks?!
------ Ah "humanity" -- fight on, fight on!' -- for it's the fulfillment of the Bible -- as Jesus said.- "There needs to be wars." (It more reassuringly confirms my thoughts of how much we're going to appreciate Heaven when we get there: "No more tears, no more sorrows!") ---- The damned war -- it took all my paternal- Uncles, except the last one, Marklen, who was too young to go. -- And it made widows of all my Aunts! ----- I've got relatives scattered from Yerevan to Siberia, because of it! (You want to know how many Uncles? Keep reading --"you'll find out," later!)

As we traveled back through Shahoumian, Verastan, we stopped at Tamara's sister's house --- like, out in the country --- to say hello to them for a few minutes. It was dark, but Tamara coaxed me, with her eager desire to accompany her and her nephew to go into the"aigee" to pick some grapes --- just so that I can later say I was in an vineyard. We could hardly see in the dark - but fortunately, there was a little moonlight. There were trenches for irrigation, and holes all around, that we almost stepped into, and we laughed like a couple of kids with our silly behavior. (At least, that's why I was laughing. -- Maybe she was trying to have me fall in a ditch?!) But, really -- it was nice to have a few moments of abandoned laughter -- to get some life back into us after sitting in a car for a few hours, and only talking about serious, matter-of--fact, and sometimes, sad topics. But, we managed to pick a few grapes.

    We bid them farewell, and they were displeased to have us go so soon. - They wanted us to sleep overnight; but the cabbie had to be home by 1:00 A.M. for the sake of his wife's worried mind, over his driving, through the mountains) And I don't blame her for that -- for some places were treacherous! No road signs, no guard rails, and sometimes it even looked like "no road!") We ate grapes, and Uncle Marklen sang, as we tried to keep ourselves awake until we got back to Kirovagan at 1:00 A.M. We 'went to bed at 1:30.

September 22, Wednesday
Uncle Marklen's neighbor, in the apartment, drove us to town, and we talked with a few cab drivers until we got one that was willing to drive us to Yerevan for a mutually, agreeable price. As we traveled down the highway, I noticed a steam-roller leveling out the newly -laid asphalt -- and their highways were good ------but compared to our highways of 25 years ago. Then Uncle Marklen asked me how I liked their highway, and how fast we travelled on ours in the U.S. I told my Uncle our highways were so good that if there were no speed limits, or traffic, you could drive across the country at 120 mph without stopping: Then I noticed the cab driver started going faster, and faster - until we were going 140 kilometers (about 85 m.p.h. -- It seemed like we were going 120 mph, like a roller- coaster ride, the way we were almost leaving the road at times, because of the lack-of levelness! (It's ironic to think of my younger days, when I used to own an old, 1937 Ford that I was planning on making a roadster out of. My buddies and I had sawn and sledge-hammered the body off of it, until there was only a windshield on it, -- without a roof, fenders, or doors --

and those were the days of no seat-belts.-- And I used to fly at 90 miles an hour down the highway without ever thinking of the consequences of what might happen if I ever got a blowout on a tire. (Ah, the stupidity of youth!) --- And yet, in this Situation, of placing your life in another drivers hands, you become more cautious, and are constantly reminded of your family back home, and your responsibility to them. The drivers have more guts than brains, in Haiastan!

The driver came to a stop in a *small* village, as we drove down the Leninakan Highway, and pulled out some drinking glasses from his glove compartment and asked if we wanted a drink of "sarree joor" (mountain water) from Mount Ararat --(the mountain that all Armenians call "home.") The water was running out of pipes all along the village road, there -- and it was so cold that it froze your teeth! And it really tasted good. -- No chlorine, you know! As I drank the water, a thought comparable to the U.S. National Anthem went through my mind-- "Ararat -- of thee I sing, land where our fathers died--." (How much longer must Armenians suffer, Dear God?)

There were a few places along the highway where we crossed over brick spans, that were built over small riverbeds, which looked like architecture from the Roman Empire days. (And I imagine there may be some reality there, since Roman royalty had married Armenian maidens during Biblical times, and later.) Interspersed along the highway, there were remains of ancient churches which seemed to be the only structures left that attested to the existence of Christian communities of centuries past. At some points, not too remote from Yerevan, I noticed homes built into the ground -- with only two feet of the house-and- roof above ground. At great intervals - and at major points along the highway, there were uniformed patrols, armed with machine-guns, standing by modern, but small buildings. We finally got back to Yerevan, to Ovsanna's and, as usual, my Aunt came over to greet me. They had butchered the lamb (really, a ram, with horns) that they had bought for my birthday (tomorrow) and planned on a "Madagh" (a celebration, thanking God for my blessed occasion.) We went to the Ani hotel (where I was supposed to be boarding) and took a shower. We went back to Ovsan's and told them we were going to look at the stores in town. (I wanted to have more opportunity to see the city life, and its functions.) Marklen, Tamara and their son Aramais, and Yura-and-I walked down to the main street and caught a streetcar going into the business district. They had women conductors! We looked around and compared prices at different stores. I noticed most men didn't display any courtesy toward the women -- like stepping aside and allowing a female to walk past, at narrow parts of the walks, or to hold a door open for them, and especially to stand up and allow a lady to have their seat. Hours later, when we got back to my Aunt's house, the women were still cleaning the meat off of the bones, and washing the intestines of the ram -- and my cousin's child was playing with the intestine that was blown up, like a balloon!! It was like solid rock around the outside of my Aunt's house, and my Aunt was banging the ram's head against the ground, while in a squatting position. (I didn't understand what this was all about, till I got home and asked my mother about it. And she laughed, then said: "That's the way they knock the worms out of the sheep's nose -- they breed in there. -- And when they're done, then, they cook the head.") They scraped every bit of meat off of the bones, and worked until it got dark. (American-women -- count your blessings!) There were more relatives who had come from out of town to visit me. We had cognac and "rahkhi" -- and went to bed about 1:00 A.M.

September 23rd: Thursday, 1971 -----My 45 birthday!
    I was awakened at 7:30 A.M. (on the front porch) to meet a couple more of my relatives who had just arrived. As we were sitting there at the dining table, waiting for breakfast, we had a couple of drinks, greeting, each other -- and Tamara came in with a bouquet of flowers for me, gave me a kiss, and wished me a happy birthday. Then she took my hand, and displayed a gold ring that she had bought me, and put it on my finger. (AND,

A6AIN: How embarrassing it was for me -- I was the one who had the money - at least more than they had - and they were giving "me" gifts! It was a delicate position to be in -- you try to refuse graciously, without hurting their feelings -- yet, you accept, knowing they can't afford it, but know it is what makes them happy! I thought it wise to accept and repay my gratitude by sending them things after I got back in the "States.") I told her that I already had a wedding band and couldn't think of removing it -- and she said she'd like to have me wear her ring also, as a remembrance of my birthday, with my relatives in Armenia. ---So, now I have two wedding bands on, and when people ask me about the rings, I tell them: "I married my Uncles wife in Armenia'" -- and crack up laughing at their expressions! Naturally, I tell them what really happened. Seriously, though, it reminds me of all my fond memories of Armenia, and now I feel married to it.

As Aunt Ovsan brought piping-hot soup to the table, she asked: "Have you ever had 'khash,' before?" I said-. "No." My cousins immediately said: "It's the best thing you can eat for breakfast." (Don't forget; an Armenian "A" is pronounced as "ah." -- Of "Khash" --ugh! It was the intestines, gizzards, skin and meat from the lamb's (ram) head, boiled in water!! Who said Armenians didn't have SOUL-food?! Well-before I arrived, I had resolved myself to eating everything they ate, and I wasn't going to go back on my word -- so I ate it! (But if someone in the States asked me to eat it, I wouldn't have, even for a million dollars.) -- I was feeling pretty good from the cognac, by this time anyway, so it didn't really matter. My relatives added broken pieces of bread and garlic to theirs --wow. As we ate, I kept jotting notes down in my notebook, and when they asked me what I was writing, I told them: "I'm going to write a book on how I became a "beyoneets" (a"drunkard" be-yon-eets) in 18 days!" -- and they all laughed, hilariously.   They drank booze like "Americans" drink coffee!) Later on, we went into town (Yerevan, and when we got back, a few of my relatives were walking around outside, and I felt something was wrong ------ After inquiring, we were informed that

Tamara's gold necklace was lost in the sewer-drain, and may have become lost, or lodged underground -- from the house to the drainage ditch about 200 feet away, that ran behind the house. --- And how it got lost was another story! --- Tamara was washing her hair, along with a few articles of clothing she was washing in a large vat on the floor, out on the front porch.-- And as she was bent over, her necklace slipped over the top of her head and fell into the tub -- and she knew it. -- But since she was in a hurry to go grocery shopping before everyone woke up, she just left it in the tub, feeling she'd get it after she came back from shopping and finished washing her clothes. My second- cousin, Marietta (13) wanting to be helpful, finished washing the clothing and dumped the water into the drain. ----- Goodbye, gold-necklace!

So, here was Tamara, standing in the drainage ditch, up to her ankles in slime, and my cousin had a long clothesline wire in the sewer-pipe, fishing for the necklace, and my other relatives were pouring water in the drain from the other end, trying to wash it down. My Uncle Marklen, after hearing what happened, got frustratingly irritated with his wife's negligence (because she had lost one before, due to her casualness) and told her to forget about it -- saying it was a lost cause, and you're wasting your time. - Then he told me: "Let's go in and play some "nardi" (backgammon), it's too hot out here in the sun." After hearing how much the necklace cost ($1,500.00), I wasn't about to resign before an attempt in recovering it!

The necklace was fairly large and of solid gold. It made me realize the reason why all the women in town would turn their heads as we walked by. ---- I didn't think it was real. I had never seen a woman wear a thick gold chain like that before and it was, quite long! I couldn't imagine how a woman could afford such an expensive necklace when she had a barber for a husband. --- But more than that, I wouldn't have thought it possible to own such a possession while living in the Soviet Union! For devious reasons, I would have thought they would have confiscated it from her! But

Uncle Marklen was a good-natured person, and money didn't seem to have any influence on him, so I imagine he let her have anything she desired. What the hell, you couldn't buy an automobile, and other than the necessities in life, what could you spend your money on? -- They didn't provide all the unimaginable things in the Soviet Union like they did in the States! This was not the Capitalist way of life -- to encourage people to spend their money on frivolous and unnecessary things! -- And that was the way they kept people from going broke -- for they had no Welfare system. -- If you didn't have money, or a job, you didn't eat!

Now, poor Marietta; she was beside her-self for causing the loss of her Aunt's necklace - although Tamara wasn't angry; quite conversely, she was sympathetic toward Marietta and felt sorry for her.

BACK TO THE NECKLACE ~~~~~~~~
Since I felt the water pressure wouldn't move it much, I took a look at the size of the drain-hole, which was about normal size, about 5 - 6 inches. So I made a ball out of rolled-up rags, but I didn't make it as big as the hole for fear I would plug up the line if in the event it hit a narrow spot. -- I didn't know what to expect; but I also, tied an additional rope-line onto it to keep one end in my hand, so if it got stuck I could at least pull it back toward me, to unplug it. I knew the water- pressure wouldn't carry a rope the 200-foot distance, so I put the string end in the hole and turned the hose on. --- Well -- that worked! The string came out the other end of the pipe! So we tied a thin rope onto the string and pulled the rope through the hole, with the string. Then I tied the ball on the end of 2 ropes, and they pulled the ball through the hole, with the other rope still in my hand. Well, the gold necklace didn't come out -- so I figured the ball wasn't big enough, and made a bigger rag-ball and pulled that one through -- all the while running water in the hole to keep the hole lubricated. Still no necklace! Well now, -- we at least know the ball isn't getting stuck -- so I told them to pull the rope faster, and if the necklace starts to move it may have more of a tendency to, keep going. Tamara is still on

the other end, in the muck, halfway to-her knees, and my cousin is pulling on the other end. And about the third time, I was getting ready to start digging! But by the fourth time, it was near the exit hole where they could reach it with the wire, and got it Out! You should have seen the neighbors standing around watching us after the word got around. -- Even the neighbors were happy for Tamara! It took us about four hours, but we were lucky. Tamara said she had a feeling in her heart that we'd get it out. I didn't tell her that I had prayed for success! -- So you see, sometimes it pays to be poor ---- otherwise I would never have had the experience of making rag balls to play baseball with when we were kids and we couldn't afford one. -- Hell, we even made our-own baseball gloves! Everybody was poor in the 1930's -- and we learned to be self-sufficient and innovative. I believe it was Socrates, who said: "Necessity is the mother of invention." And he was, right!

Later, we ate and drank, and went to visit Marklen's previous, Kirovagan-neighbor, who was now living in an apartment, here in town. He, and a couple of other Armenians from Cairo and Beirut, didn't seem pleased with their decision of moving to Armenia, because of their stringent Soviet laws. But, they were stuck, with nowhere to go!
We went back to Aunt Ovsanna's house, and more relatives had come from out of town. --There was "Serrojh" (Aunt Mariam's oldest son --my cousin) who came from Alahverdi with his wife -- (their kids had stayed home.) There was one-armed, cousin Shura and his wife, Nevart. Seyran, and Ossan-my cousin. Edvard and his wife, Anigo. Cousin Leanna and her husband/teacher, Miasnik; they are Aunt Mariam's children. Then there were three female cousins, and their husbands -- all Aunt Armenouhi's girls -- who were: Lola and Shura-who looked like a typical blond--haired Southerner; Araxie and Valod – the newest and older "Pessa"(son-in--law),- and Seeroosh and Derrenik-with the black mustache, who sang the sad songs.

My God, how was I supposed to keep track of all these names! For a guy that never had an opportunity to talk to ONE relative, and to have everybody in from all over Armenia and Georgia, it was overwhelming, to say the least! - My head was swimming in confusion! ------- And these were just a part of them. -- I didn't see all of them. We took moving pictures, out in front of the house, with my camera (which I'm glad I had brought along, so I could show my mother when I got back home) and Serrojh was acting funny; (he had a real mustache, like Hitler's.) I know it may seem insensitive describing some of the relatives, but how else was I going to try to remember them. -- Especially my dear, one-armed cousin! -- There were so many names that sounded alike, and that was bad enough! But I had to try to remember them, not really for my sake, for I never thought I'd be able to go back again -- but mainly for my mother's sake, and her fulfillment of happiness, which she was robbed of. We then played backgammon and checkers, and all the while we were playing, everyone was eating sunflower seeds -- and the ground was covered-with shells. --- They really play checkers fast and crazy, here. You "Must" jump your opponent, and when you get a King, you can go all the way across the board in one move! -- and you can even go "backwards," even before you get a King!!! It was like a combination of chess and checkers (only the King would be comparable to a chess-Queen.)

"45th" -- A Birthday of All Birthdays!'

The dinner-celebration began in honor of my birthday -- a "Madagh"-- giving praises to the Lord for this special occasion. There were at least 20 grown-ups around the dining table. The table was set for a King -- the way it looked -- but that was only the beginning. As we drank, they kept bringing more food, lamb, chicken and fish. They kept toasting me, and each time someone lifted a glass to me, I drank my drink with him, and the others did likewise. After about five or six drinks, (which was about all I was accustomed to, on special occasions -- and that's during the course of a whole evening) and this was all in about an hour. I figured I better slow down, and start "sipping" my drinks after each toast, or I'd end up drunk! I guess they realized the "obvious" by then, and my cousin Yura said it wasn't necessary for me to drink to each person's toast, that I could raise my glass each time, and wait until they went all the way around the table -- and then drink, once. --- After I'm going cross-eyed, then, he tells me! My cousin Serrojh is a man of protocol. -- He took over as Master of Ceremonies and seemed to have control of our festivities. He did a very commendable job! He knew all the formalities and procedures, and spoke with such boldness and assurance! --- He really amazed me -- for I thought he was devoid of the culture of a city man -- he looked so unmannerly and gruff at my first impression of him. (This was the epitome of the axiom, when they say: "Looks, sure can be deceiving!") He not only gained my total respect, but also my greatest sense of admiration! God, if I had his talent and demeanor, I'd have run for President of the USA.

It was hot today, and the temperature indicator they had in town read 40 degrees Centigrade! (Fortunately I did not know how hot it really was, until I got home in the U.S. and figured the temperature out by multiplying 40 C. by 1.8 F. and adding 32 F., to find out it was 104 Fahrenheit that day! (Don't ask me how I knew that -- I just played with the figures long enough until I came up with that formula. -- And I must say, it's easier to remember and calculate, than the method presently used.) No wonder all the men had their shirts off at the dinner table! I tried to maintain a dignified composure, and sweated with my shirt on, even after their encouragement to remove it. (And, "NO," dear reader, I am not the 98 pound weakling that they advertise in Charles Atlas' literature! Although, I used to be, when I was 15 --and took-up weight lifting and bodybuilding, and could bend a 60-penny nail with my hands -- which is a nail about the size of a wooden pencil.
The dinner lasted about 3-1/2 hours. They ended by toasting my aunts and my Uncle Marklen. They sang and laughed. Then I was asked to say something, and although I am not a speechmaker, I

felt if there ever was an occasion to say something, this was the most called for, special moment in my life. I thanked them for their warm and profound reception of me, and for their expressions, and remarked that: "I had never had a party like this in all my life -- nor, had I ever seen one like it!" I said: "My heart had finally found rest -- after waiting 45 years to see my mother's place of birth -- my Grandparents' graves, and was sorry I hadn't had the opportunity to see them before they died. I wanted so much to hold my mother's mother in my arms, to kiss her and thank her for giving me a mother, like I have. She's the best mother in the world, and when they see her when she comes, 'they're' going to be doing the crying." (Because I was crying as I spoke, and most of them were in tears listening to me pour my-heart out to them.) It was really heart breaking to hear the way they made toasts to the memory of their loved ones! (Here, in the United States" we can't wait long enough to bury someone - like mass production -- and forget about them. But in Armenia, it seems they cherish their memories. And even if someone might say it may-be an excuse in order to drink more, I would have to say, I'd rather see it their way, than ours! They endear their memories. -- "That's, Heritage!" -- Their way of life!

As the hours passed, everyone was feeling the effects of the alcohol. I was so light-headed and tired, that, I was giddy and couldn't stop giggling because of the way Serrojh kept going on and on with his reminiscent and nostalgic toasts. They would talk for five or ten minutes at a time! (This is a day I shall never forget!--How much more of an Armenian can you be, than to be in Armenia with Your relatives?! I thanked God with a very humble heart that night, as I laid on Yura's hand-made wooden-bed, outdoors.

September 24th: Friday

It's now 7:30) A.M. --- and the kids are up and crying, while the women are cleaning up! One of the children (Maretta's son) is now standing in the doorway, out front, and is going "cheesh" (urinating) on the ground.--- It's just like in the movies. (I must

explain here, "this" Maretta is not my 2nd cousin -- this one is Ovsanna's daughter-in-law, and they share the same house: the two brothers, Yura, Jura-and-his- wife--Maretta--and two kids, and Aunt Ovsan.) It seems they hadn't been living here too many years, since Aunt Ovsan retired after 25 years of picking grapes in the vineyard, for the collective Soviet government, in her hometown of Shoulaver, Georgia and moved to Yerevan after her boys were released from incarceration. And the boys were building this home for their mother, to provide her with some joy in life after all the heartaches they had caused her. And they were like one family-- all loving the kids. And Maretta was another nice, sweet girl. But my Aunt "Ovsan" -- you couldn't find anyone more altruistic than her!! She was giving her life for her "family." And, in the process of building a home for their mother, the boys would always seem to manage in bringing home building materials to add on to the house. It seemed it was a "Soviet trait" with the needy masses ---- they were 'all' "ripping-off" the system -- just like the system was ripping them off!! The Armenian terminology "goghootiun" would be apropos, here! In fact, that's probably how the whole neighborhood was going up! I guess you could say it was the Armenians against-the-Russian oppression. -- And the Russians were sucking all the blood, sweat and wealth from all the States under their domination, and tried to convince them it was all for the good of the Union! As long as the Kremlin bosses had all their puppets in place, giving them positions of superiority, and a better life, and had their 'Armenian stooges' spying on their own Armenian-people, why wouldn't you expect the poor masses to respond in a resentful, arbitrary manner?! What the Russians seemed to overlook was, the centuries-old, past history of the little race of Armenian people, who had built-in-genes of succeeding in resisting-domination from all the preceding powers that tried to dominate
them. It was "Little Armenia" who, through the centuries, acquired all the knowledge from each dominant nation that tried to make it succumb through its will! --- It was "Little Armenia" that provided more Generals to the Soviet Army than any of the other States. It

was "Little Armenia" who gave the life of 1/4 of its youth to the World War Two effort, when promised by Russia's biggest, conniving, treacherous, prevaricator -Joseph Stalin- that Armenia would receive its Armenian-"Karabakh" lands back after the war!! --- Another story? - And to think -- I started with "Cheesh"!

So here's little 'Aramo' "cheeshing" outside, and his Grandmother Ovsanna saw him and asked, in an admonishing tone: "Aramo, what are you doing?" -- She didn't even get angry. You couldn't help but note the difference in lifestyles. -- They didn't seem to be living under pressure, and exuded a more relaxed atmosphere. (Sort of comparable to my philosophy: If you can't do anything about a Situation, after you've tried to do everything possible -- then don't worry about it. ---- No sense getting ulcers over things you can't control.)

My cousins and I played a little "Narrdi" (backgammon) before breakfast was served. -- As usual, cognac, before breakfast! They say it's good for the appetite! (A previous night, I was told that if you have a bite to eat after every drink, it'll keep you from getting sick. --- This must be their secret to heavy drinking!) In the afternoon, we walked around town, and then I had to excuse myself from my relatives in order to attend the I:00 P.M. (compulsory) dinner celebration with the other tourists in our group, at the Hotel Ani.

The man in charge of the Armenian-Americans had lived in the USA for some time. He indulged in the social amenities prior to acquainting himself to the opinions of the various personalities. He queried whether we were pleased with our "Sossie" (lady guide's name) and received a responding applause. Then he introduced her fiance, sitting next to her (who must have been a "party member" also, or he wouldn't have been wearing a Suit! -- Or possibly Wouldn't have been in attendance!) Then he asked if we had visited the various sites and what we thought of them. From Our group, he asked a woman -- Varsenik Caloustian (a widow, from California) and me, to give a little speech. --- Me?! I'm certainly not a speechmaker! And I can't imagine why he chose "me"! (Note: to my dear readers: In retrospect, after I thought about this for a while, I came to realize that was why God had all of my relatives making speeches for me--"He" was training me for this occasion! - Bless You, Father, for Your Divine Mysteries!) --- Anyway -- I told them my Armenian wasn't as good as I would like it to be, but I'd try. I told them how I had known of my long-lost relatives in Armenia; but, had it not been for my (13 weeks, paid) "vacation" - ("hankeest" 'rest', as some say; but properly should be "artsagoort") -- that I had been entitled to, for being a Steelworker, that I never would have had the opportunity to fulfill a lifelong and "impossible" dream' -- I said: "It was a happy occasion for me to be able to see my mother's place of birth, and the home where she was born- and still standing. That it had been over 50 years since my mother left Armenia, and that I had told my relatives, jokingly, that if my mother didn't come next year (1972,) that I would break her arms." (They all laughed.) -- I spoke about the beauty of the country, and Yerevan; and I mentioned that there were some bad things I saw that I didn't like (to let them know that the Soviet Union wasn't "Heaven" -- as some of the Armenian-American communists tried to make everyone believe!   But, in all fairness to the Soviet Union (as I tried to be diplomatic) there were things in our country (USA) that were bad, also. I spoke of my father who had departed from this world (in 1949) -- and that it was so unreal to see his brother, who looked just like him. I told them, with all the tears that we shed, I couldn't wait to come back -- I liked it so much. They applauded my expression of thoughts, and we drank a glass of wine to toast this happy and memorable occasion.

    I walked around town later with my cousins and we came back to Aunt Ovsanna's for supper. Cousin Davit and his wife "Svetta" came over again about 10:30 P.M. We went back to the hotel at 11:30. My Aunts had packed my suitcase with gifts and cognac -- it must have weighed 50 pounds -- without my clothes in it!! I tried to tell them not to put any liquor in my bags, and that I would pack my own suitcase --- but they insisted, and would have it no other way! Well, I felt if Customs asked me, I'd just tell them the truth -- and if I went to Siberia, I could see another cousin of mine, who lived there.

September 25th: Saturday
Got up at 6:OO A.M., and after breakfast, went down to the lobby with my cousins Yura and Aramais who assisted me with my luggage. (Can you imagine, my cousins being there at 6?! How many American-Armenians would inconvenience themselves like that for their relatives?! I can imagine most of them would be grumbling, if they "did!" ---- And my cousin Yura, Ovsanna's son -- I just couldn't believe how much he must have inconvenienced himself for the time that I was there. But it seemed no matter what, or when, he was always there to be of assistance, or entertainment -- always availing himself for me -- and that was the reason he took his vacation time off from work, just for me! I don't know how I can ever repay him. -- But, God willing, I know the day will come! -- And I shall never forget -- none of them!) I had to take the bus to the airport, and the relatives said they wanted to see me there. Waiting for the plane's preparation and transferring of luggage from the bus was quite an awkward ordeal. -- Not knowing the appropriate words to say to my relatives while we waited -- the feeling of sadness overcoming me, increasingly, as I became more aware that my departure was not a dream, and wondering if I'd ever really see my relatives again. The tension, mounting, as the time passed, and I was getting sadder by the minute. One of the girls (Marietta) was crying --- (How could anyone with a heart not be overcome with such affection) -- as she gazed up at me so lovingly, and it almost made me cry. (I didn't consider myself so precious that anyone would cry over my departure.) The airline's passenger-bus came to transport us onto the field, to the waiting plane --- and as we kissed goodbye, my aunts (my mother's three sisters) repeatedly reminded me of

insisting upon my mother to come next year (1972,) as I had promised them.

As we left Yerevan (Russianized, to "Erevan"), we once again saw the black, 17,000-foot-high mountain of "Ararat"--and a nostalgic feeling overcame me. My thoughts ran through all my chain of events --- from the time I had left home, till, now. -- And in the anguished and emotional state that I felt in those few seconds, I couldn't help but have tears in my eyes -- for God must have truly blessed me for this unbelievable opportunity. -- And I thanked him with an adjoining question as to when He would give "our Ararat" back to the Armenians.

We landed in Moscow, in the early afternoon, and they took us by bus to the Hotel Metrapole. It was really modern (air conditioning, good elevators, escalators to the dining area on the 2nd floor, etc.) But I noticed, again, the theft-proof system: A woman at the desk near the elevators, whom you got your room-key from as you came onto your floor, and returned to, when you left your room. We went to the "American dollar" store, there. We took the subway for a short ride, and it has New York and London subways beat, by far. -- For 5 cents you can cross the city. The view from the hotel room was quite an experience! ---- As I looked out at the 11-lane boulevard, I couldn't help but notice how it seemed to diminish the flowing traffic by its enormity. I watched an uniformed policeman in the center lane, and heard him blow his whistle at a passing car. The driver hit his-brakes as if he was making an emergency stop --- by the screeching of his tires! The policeman pointed toward the curb, and the driver immediately pulled over. -- It made me smile to think how ineffectual a police whistle would have been in the "States." They certainly don't fool around in Russia!!

Later, as I walked the sidewalks below, I observed a similar performance -- so, the first time was not an isolated case. -- The police are respected -- or feared! (And the same policy in the States would be beneficial for our overly permissive and liberal society, if it expects law and order to be maintained with dignity!)

That evening, after dinner, I was invited by Richard "Hratch" Tashjian, a friendly, Massachusetts tourist, to meet his artist friend living in Moscow. (There are 300,OO0) Armenians living in Moscow.) He took us to a "stand-up" (no chairs) doughnut and coffee shop, and insisted he pay, although he was having financial difficulties! He looked like a typical, liberated-American painter -- with beard and casual garb. He was soft-spoken, sincere, polite, well mannered and sympathetic toward the Armenian cause. Later, he took us
(request) to the Armenian Community in the city, and we walked down "Armenia Street" in the dimly- lit night. He tried to introduce us to some of his friends there, but they weren't in. He gave us some background information of the area, and took us to the Lazarian Academy (Armenian Artist's Institute) down the street. And it was so dimly lit that I thought we'd get arrested for 'suspicion of burglary' as we ducked our way through the shrubs to get into the courtyard. There was a large statue of Lazarian (one of the Lazarian-brothers who founded the building) --- and at its base was a plaque inscribed with some memorabilia, and he read it for us by the light of a flickering match.

The building was quite impressive with its carved marble pillars. It must have really been quite a productive Center in its day. He told us the story of how the Russians tried to minimize and obliterate its importance by allowing the "Severruh-oo (Blacks-and) Japonatsi-neruh"(Japanese) to take control of it and run it into the ground. He also told us how the Armenians in the community became irate and indignant about its negligence and disrepair, and how they produced a document given to them, from Lenin, which-stated that the property and the building shall always belong to the Armenians! They regained control of the building, and are now in the process of rejuvenating it.
As we got out of the taxi-cab, back at the Hotel Metrapole, the artist, "Hratch" (name with held in first edition, for security purposes) gave the artist some money before stepping out of the

cab. And the artist was overcome with Hratch's generosity and stepped out of the cab to firmly embrace him in expressing his emotional appreciation, before our friendly departure. It was quite touching; they both had tears in their eyes. Isn't this the way all "Hye's" should act toward each other? Helping each other out -- putting our personal ideologies aside in the time of need -- and venting our frustrations out on the Turks, instead of each other?

Septem6er 26th: Sunday, 1971
We left the Hotel Metrapole before noon and arrived at the Moscow Airport. --- We had to get our passports back from the Russians (they take possession of them -- and you don't get it back until you're leaving the country! They make sure everybody coming into the Soviet Union comes into Russia first, so they can reap more money from the tourists while visiting relatives in their satellite countries. But then, again, I guess you could say it may- be a reassurance that you do leave the country alive, for, now, you- have two Countries responsible for your safety, if in the event you do surreptitiously disappear for some nefarious reason, along with your money!) And (compulsory) exchanged all of our "Russian" Currency before we left the country. The airport is quite elaborate, and enormous. As we waited, I had to "go"! -- So, I looked at the picture of a man on the wall leading down the stairs, to the toilet, which was about 50 feet square. --- And I was stunned to see an elderly woman mopping the floor, as the men relieved themselves --- Oh, well, "When in Rome -------- (You sure can't tell your kidneys to forget it!) We were delayed so long that our plane was ready to depart -- so they didn't check our luggage on the way out!
(Some of us had time to purchase balalaikas and mandolins for less than $10.00 at the "American Dollar Store" before we were rushed on to the airplane, and left Moscow at 12:45 P.M.
After stopping at London for 1-1/2 hours, we got to New York at 7:30 P.M. The Russians had better meals on their planes, and were selling cognac on the return trip. The Russian plane rode beautifully, I must admit. (And then again, why not. -- It probably

was designed by an Armenian named "MiKoyan."-- One of their best designers, which is where their "MIG" fighter-planes got their name.) When we got into New York "Immigrations," I was amazed at difference in the security of Russia vs. USA.. They didn't even look at my bag in New York! (No wonder dope gets into the country!! ---- But, then again, I guess Our Immigrations felt that no one would be that stupid to try to smuggle drugs through Russia -- or they would end up in "Siberia!") ---- But, on this trip, we weren't checked on either end! -- And that's how things get through! Some people will do anything for money!! I still have my "declaration slip" that someone neglected to collect -- even though I was legitimate!

As I got back to Detroit Metropolitan Airport, all of my loved ones were there to greet me! -- You'd think they were welcoming the President!! I contained my emotions until I reached my mother, but I couldn't hold back the flooding tears of happiness-and-heartbreak, as I embraced her. --- It was like returning back to Mother Earth from a trip to outer space! -- dying, to tell everyone what it was like, and yet so emotional to be back from a trip you thought you would never survive, not from the fear but the impact of every emotion on your senses, that I was choked up, quivering from sorrow and happiness, and couldn't talk. --- This was the second point of my trip that I thought I was going to fall into the sea of insanity!

I couldn't wait to tell my mother of the love and tribulations that I had felt and seen. I think I had made this trip for my mother's sake, as much as for mine -- to help fulfill the void of family life she must have missed, living here, in the U.S.A. -- and for mine, to know what it was like to have relatives! Some thing some people take for granted! Some thing the Turks stole from Millions of Armenians! -------

"Talaat," -- May you burn, in, Hell !

Written: 12-26-76 Essay Page: 4
Excerpt of: Ovsanna's Grapes

An ode to Aunt Ovsan
Singing Upon the Winds
Rest gently my sweet Aunt
And listen to my fond remembrances
For they shall keep you warm
As they echo from Mt. Ararat.
If everyone could have had
Such a pure heart as yours
The world would flow with love
With no more wars to be fought.
And yet, with this kind of love
There would be no more sorrows endured
By those who are, left behind,
More fond remembrances,
Being brought to mind.
Let me sing upon the winds
And hope that God may hear
The Hosannah's I shout of Him
For my Dearly, departed Aunt.
Rest gently, Dear Ovsan, rest gently.
Sooren Simon Apkarian, Poet: S. P.
(I shall cry for you till my dying day.)
    Menchev mernelous oruh yes kez guh heshem

    Act 2: Four years later
Prologue to: September ---- 1975
After my first trip to Armenia -----------
My mother looked at all the pictures and movies that I had taken in 1971, and for whatever reason it was, she made her first trip to Armenia ---- the next year!
For years she had said, she had made a vow to never go back, because her Aunt had tricked her and married her off to my father while her parents weren't at home. --- He probably bought her for a few chickens and a cow -- who knows?! Because my father never told us about his parents, my father's brother "Avo" told me that my father had left home when he (Avo) was about 11 years

old. My father was 14 years older than him (and 15 years older than my mother.)

(Momentary interjection: filling in gaps!)
The year of 1915, was the major thrust of the Turks, regarding the "Armenian Genocide." Unfortunately, Germany had intents of declaring, war in Europe and was training and supplying the Turks as their ally --- and the Turks took advantage of this situation by using the Armenians as their training ground, and also resolving their problem with the Armenian Question. It's ironic to think that the Turkish government had important governmental positions being handled by more capable and intelligent people, as the Armenians, and yet undermined their own financial progress, by killing off all the Armenian officials, because of their jealousy of the industrious and business-minded Armenians! This was the beginning of the world's blackest page in history -- the 20th Century's "Genocide of the Armenian race-." The annihilation of .1,457,231 innocent men, women and children!! -- "Half" of the Armenian race!! They were worried that the Armenians would eventually govern the whole country. If Turks had only known how much better off they would have been'! And for 50 years their own people have been suffering in their backwardness and ignorance, while the European countries seem to turn their backs on people whom they consider uncivilized --- and yet, were the ones who turned a blind eye toward Turkish genocidal machinations and its resolution. --- And "these" were supposed to have been "Christian" countries?! ---- You hypocrites should have all perished during the Crusades!! For you are-an-abomination of such a title! If Christians had helped each other half as much as the Jews help each other, this whole world Would have been Christianized, by now!! -- Do I hear you muttering, now?" Oh, if that angers you -- listen to this! I'm going to enlighten YOU to one of Jesus' parables! -- Now take a deep breath so you don't choke! Remember- Jesus saying:"--- for the first shall be last, and the last shall be first."? -- Yes!' Armenia

will be there on the right hand side of God, as you approach Jesus to be judged!!

(Back to the story
Sometime between 1915 and 1919 my father had been in San Francisco,
California. Unfortunately, I had never asked him how he ever got there. But I presume he must have gotten there on a Russian freighter, since the Russians had their influence in that part of our country; because they used to own Alaska and sold it to United States for 7 million dollars, 20 years before my father was born!
I understand my father tried to join the Army when World War One was declared, but they rejected him because of a missing index on his trigger-finger and couldn't-fire a gun with his right hand.

It seems that, even today, if you mention "America" to someone on the eastern side of the Atlantic, the first word that comes out of their mouths is "California!"--And, I imagine, that's where my father wanted to go to get rich: On the streets of San Francisco, where the word of "gold" stirred the imaginations of everyone since the gold-rush days (1849). I imagine Russian freighters knew the course by heart -- West-South-West, from the Mediterranean to the Gulf of Mexico! And my old man was probably a part of the crew, paying his way to California. Well, anyway, there he was, looking for gold, but it wasn't found on the streets like he had thought -- the only gold he saw was on the gilded edges of dishes, in a restaurant -- he became a dishwasher! Well, what the hell did you expect?' The U.S. Government wasn't giving out college tuitions at that time! But, hey! Don't laugh. He at least "worked" for a living! -- And that's more than you can say for most of the immigrants who come into the Country today.-- Now-a-days they sign up for- welfare as soon as they get off of the plane! --They didn't even have to take a ship!

I don't know how long he stayed in California -- but he sure got "rich!" -- At least by the standards of country folks -- for by the time he got to my mother's home town of Shoulaver, Shahoumian, Georgia, he had a suitcase full of money! -- Of Course they may have all been One Dollar bills -- but who the hell knew the difference in Georgia?! They must have thought he was a multi-millionaire!

My father did have a sense of humor, I must say. From hearing the story of how my mother put it -- it sort of reminds me of the old Charlie Chaplin movies -- for my mother said he used to pour the money on the floor and rub his feet through it, like it was nothing! And to think of the grandiose cock-and-bull story he handed her, telling her when she married him that her pretty, little hands would never touch dirty dishes! -- Little did she realize that she would be pulling a plow on a Pennsylvania farm, because they couldn't afford a horse! And to think my mother used to laugh about it -(in retrospect)- saying: "I was young and stupid." -- She had probably just turned 17 when my father married her. My dear old mother ---- She had told us that she didn't want to marry our father, because he was almost twice her age -- 15 years older than her -- and that she had shaved all the hair off of her head to dissuade him --- but he still married her.

My uncle Avo told me that his mother had starved to death because of the Turks. And by 1918, he had joined the Russian army. I guess he had no choice -- the damned Russians had come into Armenia by acting like they were going to help the Armenians, but it was just a pretense in order to get a foothold on the border of Turkey, their virtual enemy. Since my father couldn't go back to his town of Shirak, Armenia -- because the Turks had driven all the Armenians out of about 80% of Armenian lands, and the Russians were controlling the last 20% of Armenia, he decided to move back to "America." Shirak is just across the border from Leninakan, by the "Baiyandour" River.

Since the greatest majority of Americans and probably most Europeans -- are ignorant of Armenian history I should like to point out, for the sake of objectivity and enlightenment, that Armenia originally, in size, would have been comparable to twice the size of Italy, or half the size of France. -- That's over 120,000 square miles -- and today, it may amount to 20,OOO square miles. --- Where the hell is the justice, "World?!"' -- "Where?! -- ----
And do you remember this saying: "Whatever you did for the least of them, you also did unto me." May this saying sear into Your minds, you hypocrites of the United Nations!!

I Suspect my father never told us about our paternal grandmother being starved to death, so that we wouldn't go through life with hate in our hearts! He didn't want to burden us with a lifelong bitterness toward the Turks about making restitution, for he knew the deaf world wasn't going to listen to our plea. -- Armenia didn't have anything the world could prosper from!
And to those "Christian" minded people who preach the Gospel, about forgiving your enemy --- I have only one thing to say to them: "The Turks never asked for forgiveness!" -- And if they "did," ask -- I would have to forgive them. --- For I "know" what God, said about forgiveness!

My grandmother's starvation by the Turks was probably the reason why my father was a member of the Armenian Revolutionary Federation. And I only found that out from my mother, years after he passed away. Looking back on my youth finally made me realize what all the comings-and-goings of strange men into our house was all about! As I got older and learned more about A.R.F. I became aware of the name of another well known man in the organization, who's name was "Tandourjian" which I had become accustomed to hearing during those meetings of strangers, with my father. At least I knew my father didn't die without trying to help the Armenian cause. That's more than I can say for those Armenians who got engulfed in the quagmire of assimilation! To me, those were the rootless people who didn't pass on the heritage of Armenia to their children. --- And in the good ol' U.S.A. the Pilgrims' descendants sing the song about:-- "Land where our fathers died, land of thy pilgrims' pride!" --- But what about "Armenian" children's pride --- where is "their" land, where their fathers died?! --- The land that used to be called "home" over three thousand years ago!

Then, there was this Russian Armenian man, named "Ashot," a friend of my mother, who used to mock my father because he was an A.R.F. member, and whenever he would see my two older brothers and I coming home (from playing baseball) he would always say "khod varroghnerruh yegon!" (grass-burners are coming) -- which was in reference to the Armenian "fedayee" soldiers who would burn the grass, or wheat behind them, while retreating from the Turks, so they wouldn't leave anything behind for them to eat! My mother in her infinite wisdom, I guess, felt it was probably best not to tell me of these things until I was mature enough to utilize proper discretion.

Even though I am considered of Russian-Armenian descent, some may wonder why I should feel such fervor toward "Armenianism." --- Armenians all over the world, no matter where they are born, are descendants of Armenia. To me, it doesn't matter where you are born, if you have Armenian blood in your veins, you're an Armenian!

My mother told me my great grandfather was a "Moushetsi" (from Moush) -- who emigrated to Verastan (Georgia.) Just like a salmon travelling back upstream to lay its eggs, and die, humans follow the same course of nature -- if not physically, at least mentally. Everyone has a desire to know where they, came from.
There were 6 children in our family. I was the only one who didn't get assimilated. (Sorry, Uncle Sam -- but I still love you!) That's a little better than 16% average. What's going to happen to the percentages in the next generations? God only knows! Anyone

who is an Armenian, who can't understand this rationale, yet, if they are Christians, should look at it from this perspective: "We" are preserving Christianity. So, in essence, for Jesus' sake, we need your love and compassion. -"Apathy" is the greatest destroyer of mankind -- not war! I want to see Armenian lands regained as much as the extremists who are killing Turks. -- But I retain my sanity by reminding myself---"Thy will be done an Earth as it is in Heaven."

....

The Year Is Now 1975 ......

It had been four years since my first trip to Armenia -- and in 1975 I was fortunate to be entitled to another 13 week "extended vacation." (Once every five years.) I was already getting 5 weeks a year paid vacation -- plus a few paid holidays. My complaint was that we were forced to work 13 out of 14 days -- and I thought that was slavery! Where the hell were my rights to "freedom?!" --- But 13 weeks of paid vacation?' I thought that was ludicrous" How long did these people think we were going to stay in business, and compete with foreign labor, when they were giving away the company store'!

In 1968 I wrote critical letters to the Corporate President and my International Union President - of the United Steelworkers of America, and told them how stupid I thought it was agreeing to such an outrageous proposal, because I felt it would put a lot of Steelworkers out of work. Would you "believe," the Corporate President answered my letter, but my own Union didn't respond! Immature minds don't concern themselves about the consequences; they have the "sev" mentality! Everybody wants something for nothing! But, "Hey," I wasn't going to turn it down! If we're all on the same ship in the middle of the ocean and these dummies want to sink the ship -- hell, I might as well get my "kef" too. (kef = enjoyment.)

Well, my mother and I had made plans to go to Yerevan this year, so we went. We drove to Toronto, Canada and hooked-up with the Beirut-Armenians (referred to as "Beirutseez", spelled

Beirutsis) who were also booked by the Sevan Travel Agency. We left Toronto and arrived in Montreal 45 minutes later. In Montreal, we boarded a Russian Aeroflot plane and it took us a little-over 8 hours to get to Paris, France. There were quite a few French people on this flight. After we left Paris, we arrived in Moscow 3- 1/2 hours later. During the flight, we had some of the Communist-Party Frenchmen on board. Their typical authoritarian attitude was no different than the Russians'! -- They don't ask the stewardesses for service-- they demand it! This was my second time on a Russian plane, and I must admit, their service is better. They are -far more business--like and the stewardesses are pleasant but they don't smile as much, yet are more efficient. --I'm somehow left with the feeling that if they don't perform-well, they won't have a job!

I was sitting next to a German, and although our verbal communication was difficult, we managed to "converse" by drawing pictures and writing figures in my notebook. We informed each other of our vocations and wages. He related that he was a computer- engineer, computerizing machinery for automation. I was humored by this, thinking about the letter that I had written to my International Union President about foreign competition, and this guy is drawing X's over machine-operators' bodies -- showing me how his job is going to eliminate workers! He wrote how he was travelling to the USA, Britain, France, Poland and the USSR He indicated that he would get 5 days per week vacation pay-for 4 weeks, a year, and I showed him that I received 6 days per week, for 5 weeks per year. He asked me how much I would make in a month, and when I wrote it down on paper, he showed me he was making about two-thirds (2/3) of my wages. When I wrote this on paper, how much an engineer of his ability could be making in the "States" he just shook his without saying a word, and looked sad. I don't believe-in deceiving people by exaggerating, like some "Americans" like to brag. Nor do I like to hurt their feelings. But, facts are facts. But one thing is certain. If you don't talk to people, you'll never learn anything! -- And I felt "truth" was a good way for Americans to undermine "Communism!" They deserved a better life!

Well, we finally got to Moscow. And guess what? -- No overnight stops! We were told that we were going to catch the next plane to Armenia. By the time we arrived in Yerevan we had logged about 14 hours of flying time -- and everybody was exhausted. Like that wasn't bad enough, we had to spend over an hour waiting until they found some of the luggage they couldn't find in the warehouse. And then, they still didn't find it all. One poor woman was without luggage for about two weeks before they found it. This is not the U.S., folks! And one thing that you learn fast is, don't complain as though you were in the States, or you'll have more trouble!

For "civilized" people, we "Americans" sure lose our sense of respect real quick. No one seems to remember that they are in a foreign country. -- No patience! If you are the complaining type of person -- stay home. You could end up in Siberia just by creating an argument with the officials. -- And who are the "officials?" Anyone with any authority, whatsoever! Even the hotel manager! They are polite, as long as you are polite and show respect. But you must remember to restrain your American independence and free-speech mentality! The Armenian officials are even more strict, because they see the way the Americans splurge, and I'm sure they subconsciously resent us; just like any other country would that lacks a life of abundance.

By the time we arrived at the Hotel Ani, my head was ready to split! Fortunately they didn't take too long assigning us to our rooms, so by the time I got my mother situated, taking her luggage to her room, I took a couple of aspirins and went to bed. I had gone about 40 hours without sleep. You become used to those things, being a steelworker and working different shifts and weekends. But when it's a situation you don't have control over-, it makes it more difficult. --- It is now 2400 hours (12 a.m.).

September 13th:

It is now morning ......

My mother called me at 10:00 A.M. (They had told us last night that since we arrived late, we would have a late breakfast.)-- "Dugha jon, zartoon-ess?!" ("Son dear, are you awake?") My mother said, as I answered the phone. --At 49 years of age, it was still the sweetest words a guy could hear -- "dugha jon!" -- my mother's sweet voice! After I hung up, a strange feeling came over me. -- Now it was my Armenian mother's voice -- in Armenia! On the foreign soil that the Turks had deprived me of being born on! I sat down, from the lack of containment -- my emotions overflowed-- and the tears came flowing from my eyes. (Fortunately, I prefer writing about God and Jesus, otherwise I would have had thousands of words written, cursing the Turks! -- Although I -felt like running out to the balcony and screaming epithets at the Turks, my civilized thoughts restrained me, knowing that "Jesus" knows best. That "One word" the Turks hate!)

Well, we picked the right day (or was it the wrong?!) Cousin Yura and Aunt Mariam met us at the stairs, as we came to the lobby of the hotel. They both met us with restrained warmth, and it was evident that there was something wrong. In the cab, on the way to Aunt Ovsanna's house, I couldn't get anymore out of them, other than Ovsanna was sick. -- But my wise mother knew. She said: "Geedem, koir'us merrods eh!" ("I know, my sister's dead!") As she said that, the tears came to my cousin Yura's eyes - as he silently pulled the black armband away from his black shirt -- confirming what my mother had said was true. Then I started to cry, silently, not wanting to add more strain to my mother's aging heart, (as the cab driver played "dodge-em" with the holes in the street that was, being re-paved.)

"Aunt Ovsanna" --- the only woman that I knew in my life that ever emanated the sweet-and-innocent essence of life! I loved her more than my sisters! (And rightly so, for she was my Aunt; - An extension of my mother!) How unfortunately, tragic. My mother's youngest sister! And she was only 6 years older than I was.

Author's note:

It is 10 years later, as I type this (1985), and I'm still crying just thinking about her! Only God could offer us a word to express her sweetness -- for humanity cannot describe it.)
Author's 2nd note: You may wonder why it took 10 years to type this. My wife misplaced my notebook, the busy little beaver that she is; can't sit still and always moving things around. And as hard as I searched to find it, it was impossible! Now here is the irony -- after I retired, which was 10 years later, I found my notebook. Just when I had all the time in the, world. --- YES -- I do believe in the Divine Mystery of life! "Our Father"-- He never ceases to amaze me.)

For all the years of deprivation and hardship this poor woman endured in her life, it is a miracle she didn't hate anything, or anyone! (Even those things that I cannot discuss in print, regarding the dominant forces!)
Yes, Aunt Ovsanna had passed away, on August 24th. Just 9 days before we arrived!
My mother's other sister, Armenouhi, and her sister-in-law, "Armen-doda" met us at the cab, as we were getting out, along with Yura's brother "Jora" and his wife Maretta. Jora was my Aunt's oldest son -- still about 10 years my junior. We silently and somberly kissed, and then began walking toward Aunt Ovsan's house, about 100 feet off of the road's entrance.
Four years had passed since I had been here last, and it wasn't difficult to see that my cousins had done remarkable progress on fixing up the house. They had an enclosed, windowed porch added to it, built by their own hands. We sat around for awhile and talked about Aunt Ovsan's passing away. --- It seems the difference in the lower altitude had an adverse effect on her; she was always remarking about how her head hurt. There may have been about 3,000 feet difference in altitude, and she couldn't get used to it.

*****(Momentary Diversion)
(Yerevan is about 2,500 feet above sea level, which isn't bad for a person from Michigan -- 400 above sea level. But having had some experience regarding altitude, I can appreciate someone's discomfort!
I took a trip to Colorado, once, and at the 8,000-foot level I wasn't bad, but at 10,000 feet I could feel the effects and discomfort. -- But when I got up to 13,000 feet-- (and we "drove up") -- I immediately got sick, light headed, weak-kneed, and felt like throwing-up and losing control of my bowels! That's how bad it can get! We had to come right back down, for I felt like I was going to die - and that may have felt better than staying there! They say: you get used to it - for my nieces, Michelle and Rene were running up and down other ridges while we were up there. But, no thanks! -- You can keep it!

My cousins, Armenouhi's-daughters came over a little later, there was more hugging and kissing, and one of them asked Yura where his wife was. Cousin Yura had gotten married about 3 months ago. His wife's name was "Venerra," 31 years old, and from the outskirts of town (which they referred to as "the country.") She was about 5 ft four inches, and weighed about 130.

My mother had made arrangements to meet some people who were relatives, of her friends in the States, and wanted me to inform them that my mother was at the Hotel Ani --- since she wasn't physically fit to be running around town, that they should come and see her. Cousin Yura said he'd show me the street. Well, as usual, it was getting dark, and here I am again, roaming around in the dark looking for people! I knocked on the door and about 20 seconds later an elderly woman answered. She was cautious
(guarded) in her conversation, and kept answering in Russian until I told her I was from 'the "United States." Then her suspicious demeanor changed, and she began talking in Armenian as she invited us in. (Maybe they thought I was from

the KGB). The apartment was beautifully furnished, with a piano, and it seemed some in-laws were visiting. They were drinking wine, and seemed like a very refined group. As I began in the social amenities. I was asked where I was from. Unfortunately, my mother hadn't told me who the people were. But, as I acquired more information from the woman (whom I had never met before), it finally dawned on me that she was the sister of some of the old friends of the family (in the States) and her brother had just passed away, not too long back. Her brother was like an Uncle to me, and I had the same name as he did. When I finally became aware of this, I couldn't help but cry, thinking, I had to cross an ocean to meet a stranger on foreign soil, to tell her about her brother's death! A brother-- whom she may, not have seen for years. It was the late Margaret Movsesian's (nee) Uncle, Sooren! She was wondering what I was crying about, and I really felt bad, thinking I had to give her the bad news. After realizing who she was, I lachrymosely embraced her and informed her of the death. ---- (How can you feel close to someone you've never met before? After she cried, she thanked me, and felt sorry for me because of the way it had affected me. (Can you imagine -- her, feeling sorry for "me"?!) She was a gracious and charming woman, withered hair, and about my age. Later, when she met my mother, she told her about the incident, as my mother informed me, with a smile. (Other than God, what greater gift can a man receive than knowing he has made his mother proud?!)

As Yura and I walked down the street, he asked me if I wanted to meet his wife. As we walked around the hospital, with Yura asking the whereabouts of his wife (a nurse) we finally found her at the maternity ward and she came outside for a minute. We kissed as we were introduced, and I could see she was quite mannerly and sort of reserved. -- More like a professional nurse, matter-of-factly, and quiet. As we walked back to Yura's, I congratulated him and asked him where he found such a beautiful girl. He informed me of some of her background and filled me in on some other private details of related verbal conflict. I tried telling him about God and love, and although God may have been listening, I'm afraid my thoughts were falling on unenthusiastic ears. Although this was in the Soviet Union, I'm afraid the fault must be placed elsewhere, for he had been incarcerated a few years during his youth, and somewhere along the line of maturation he lost his spirit. It had taken his widowed mother's life savings (and then some) to get him out of bondage. We got back to Yura's and ate and drank, and Yura got us a cab and brought me back to the hotel. I told him it wasn't necessary to come with me, but from what he conveyed, a tourist's life can be in jeopardy riding cabs at night! --- Especially if it's suspected that he has money!

Today is September 14th:
And I am up with only 4-1/2 hours of sleep. I couldn't sleep anymore. My mother said she only slept 2-1/2 hours! -- Must be jet-lag? --(No! I don't believe in that baloney! I think you just get hyped up from all the excitement. Besides, you just have so many days to stay in foreign countries, and you don't care if you don't get enough sleep. --You can catch up on it when you get home. Anyway, if you love to sleep, stay home!) After we had breakfast, my mother and I came down the hotel stairs (after waiting 5 minutes for the elevator) and we met Aunt Mariam and Yura waiting in the lobby! I don't know how they do it, inconveniencing their selves like that! I guess we have a lot to learn from these "Haiasdan" Armenians!
We went to Yura's house, and there were about 25 people there, all relatives, waiting to go to the cemetery with us. One of the relatives, my cousin's husband, was a bus driver, so at noon he came around with a bus and we were on our way to the "Gerrezmon." The highway was filled with cars, as well as the Cemetery. I didn't know it was Armenian, Memorial Day -- I thought Armenians commemorated that on April 24th! It was the first time I ever saw so many people at a cemetery at the same time! -- And I'm from "Detroit!" There were people having graves blessed all over the countryside. The Priests sure have their

hands full, here! Mom was walking slower and slower, and I asked her if she wanted to stop (3 times) for fear of the physical and emotional strain on her heart. (She already had a pacemaker). As we approached Aunt Ovsanna's grave, the other two sisters and Armen Doda (my widowed Uncle's-wife) were wailing away in unrestrained tones that could be heard a half-mile away! I took some pictures of them, and after, stood alongside my mother. After few more minutes of unrestrained hysteria, I wondered how long it was going to take my mother to take control, and, even though she had tears rolling down her cheeks she was fighting her emotions to maintain her stature. Well, I knew my mother 'well enough,' she finally stepped alongside her sisters and gently tugged on their arms, told them to stop, and in a sisterly way admonished them to gain control of themselves. They complied, passively. (At this point, as I prognosticated, I was reminded of the time, almost 25 years ago, when our father had passed away. My youngest sister "Dee," was 14 years younger than me -- and our mother told me and my two older brothers to be brave like soldiers, and not to cry! Being the disciplined offspring that we were, we complied. I never knew why she said that -- and I never asked -- but I thought it would be best for my younger brother, and sisters. --- My tears -- were in my heart! Dear ol' dad --- He didn't see 62!)

Ovsanna's two sons, Yura and Jura had initiated the ceremony by lighting candles and incense. And they had two bottles of liquor and a tray of fruit at their mother's head (area) -- and the men took turns drinking a part of each drink and spilling the rest of it onto the grave, above her head. It was something I had never seen before. My prayer was silent, in contrast to their audible chantings, and there was no use trying to say anything in Armenian that wasn't already said. I regretted they didn't understand English so they could have appreciated understanding what I was desirous of saying in a more expressive tongue. All the male relatives hadn't shaved (since it is an Armenian custom) and would only do so after 40 days. There were so many women dressed in black. It momentarily took my thoughts back to my youth, when women used to take mourning seriously, by showing more respect of their spouses. Ah, the American efficiency -- hurry-up and get-it over with!

Back at Aunt Ovsanna's house, the table was set for more than 20 people. -- And, as we drank, there were toasts to the fond memories of "Ovsan" and intonations of the future life ahead, for the dearly departed ones. I took a few more pictures, of those who I hadn't photographed before, so that I could show my brothers and sisters their "relatives." A few hours later, Yura got us a cab and we went back to the hotel. There were other people there who wanted to see my mother. It was 11:30 P.M., and after the visitors left, Yura insisted we go back to his house because, the whole clan was still there. The women were cooking for days -- and there were so many different types of food that there was no end to eating. They sure aren't like "American" women! I never once heard anyone complain about working hard. Yura took us back to the Ani hotel at 1:30 A.M. There was a doorman standing at the door -- outside -- obviously to keep watch, for there was a two-inch-thick chain, linked through the door handles! (Now, that's, "security"!)

September 15th:
This morning, Yura greeted us at the hotel lobby, along with cousin Shura's son (age 12?) from Shoulaver, Verastan (Georgia.)
My cousin "Yura" must be made out of "steel"! -- He sleeps less than I do, and he's here every morning, waiting for us! (And I thought I was a strong guy!). After we had breakfast at Yura's, we went to the cemetery again, about noon. -- Yura wanted to have the grave blessed. After the Derr Hyrr (Priest) blessed the grave, Yura asked him if it was true --- what he had heard ---- about, having the "karrasoonk" ("40 days") shortened -- and immediately, he said: "No"! Stating: "If there's 7-days in a week, and so many days in a year, why should we change the Karrasoonk? - It's

crazy! - It won't happen!" The Derr Hyrr was from Etchmiadzin, and he queried us about our country, etc. I took some more pictures of the cemetery. -- It seemed to be a new area, with plain, open fields -- with headstones engraved with picture-like simulations of the loved ones, on them.

We got back to Yura's house, and my other cousin's daughter, "Marietta" and her younger sister were there - also with Aunt Mariam's daughter, "Leanna." We exchanged affections, and later on Yura got into an argument with Leanna - about her "separation" problems from her husband. (I gathered they didn't take separation problems too lightly, here!) But, Leanna seemed to be the more liberated type of female (when I first met her in 1971) -- and I figured they were cousins, and it was more of a "family affair" -- so I didn't mitigate. But it was more like, two clashing-personalities. -- Yura's too chauvinistic!
***** (Diversion:) (But, I guess that depends on which country's perspective you're looking at it, from! -- Look where "Women's Liberation" has gotten us, here in the "States," with the divorce rate skyrocketing! Don't they believe in what it says in the Bible --- about, "The wife shall be subservient to the husband."? Maybe that's why a lot of these women quit going to church, too? And undoubtedly, why the country's going to hell! -- Boy! -- I can see the women-libbers jumping up and down after "that" remark! --- Okay, ladies! -- I was just kidding! Being a father of 3 daughters does cause me to give females more consideration. -- For the Bible also says:" The husband shall love his wife as he loves the church"! Maybe "that's" the problem -- for I see more women in church, than men! ---- Maybe that's why it rains so much -- it's God's "tears"! -- God's, sorrows'! Doesn't anybody care about God? -- Maybe I should have been a Preacher!) (Forgive me! I get carried away like that, sometimes! Who wants to listen to me, when you don't even listen to God!)

We went to the hotel and returned with some clothes-and-things my mother had brought for the children.

We returned to the hotel about a half-hour past midnight. (One of my cousin's had told me she had been required to have money to pay the doctor- for a kidney-stone operation, or he wouldn't operate! -- What kind of corruption is this? --- And it's supposed to be Socialized medicine?! Well, I guess every country has its' corruption!)

September- 16th, 1975:
Had breakfast with my mother and Helen Avedisian, a German woman, married to an Armenian. -- Every woman should be as loving and understanding as this woman! - I refrain to comment, so as not to cause her spouse embarrassment; although, you may surmise why. -- War can cause a lot of havoc in people's lives -- and sometimes there are things beyond your control!

Yura took me to his place of employment. It was a lumberyard with a small shop, where he and four other men worked, making doors and window-frames from the lumber they cut-and-planed to size. Yura introduced me to two of my second-cousins, who worked there.

We later went to a stone and cement, asphalt plant, and Yura looked for one of his relatives, to tell him something. He also applied for his vacation today -- even though he had not worked since his mother had passed away.

We later took pictures at the "sev-shuga" (called, "black-market") near his home. The market is not illegal -it's just the name they gave it. It's a market where farmers sell their goods privately (correctly called "sepagon" = which may be closer-to separate.) The other, large domed, farm-goods market was more directly controlled by the government -- called, "Bedagon" shuga. Armenia is the "California" of the Soviet Union! The fruits and vegetables cannot be excelled, that's for sure! As we walked around in the sev-shuga, which every farmer had, with his own fruit stand -- about 8 foot squares, with umbrella's covering them,

I was taking Pictures, not only of the fruit but, also of some of the intriguing features of the farmers -- who, some even looked like "Mongols." And before I knew it, some burly, belly-bulging, shirt-button-popping character comes up to me and begins gruffly asking me why I'm taking pictures, and where I'm from! (Damn! -- what the hell is this! -- a "military" installation?! Were they afraid I was going to steal secrets of their delicious looking peaches to take to Georgia, (our Peach State) in the USA? Maybe I should have told him they were "Red-necks", in Georgia, and he may have let me go? -- No offense to the Georgians, please - I love you "down-home" folks, and your pralines, too!.) --- So, as I'm trying to keep everything in low key (since I did study 100 hours of psychology at my Melvindale Library, and be "diplomatic") -- here comes my cousin Yura, to my defense, and starts raising hell with the guy! (The "Armenian Revolutionary Federation" organization is a world renown, and most "anti-Communist" organization in the world.- -- and they would have loved to have had a guy like my cousin "Yura"! ---- Because he stood right up to anyone who tried to boss him around! I mean -- as the Afro-Americans say: "In your face!" I thought he was going to make my desire of seeing my cousin, in Siberia, a reality! I heard that a man can-take a suitcase full of fruit from Yerevan to Moscow and make a profit --- even after he's paid for the air fare!)

When we got back to Yura's place -- I didn't recognize Uncle Marklen, who was standing in the doorway! He looked like a Priest, with his long, unshaven, grayish beard, and black jacket on. We hugged and kissed and his wife Tamara came out; and we hugged and kissed some more. -- Poor Uncle Marklen looked sick and drawn out. We sat at the table for lunch, and got feeling high from drinking, and crying.

Later on, mom, Marklen, Yura and I went to the airport to pick up the dozen duffel bags that we had shipped previous to our trip. They were filled with new coats that all my brothers and sisters had jointly contributed to our relatives. My mother had been widowed for 25 years, and she certainly couldn't afford much. The Archbishop happened to be passing through the airport when we arrived, and we greeted him. He was from Etchmiadzin, and we spoke for a couple of minutes. Now we had to come all the way back to the hotel, because my mother had forgotten, or misplaced the required, stamped-papers (shipping ticket for the duffel bags) that she had got approved in Moscow! My mother was upset because she was having trouble finding the papers. Well, she found the papers, and we went back to the airport. They sent us to a remote part of the warehouse, and we had to walk some distance, going through fences without gates, they were just holes, cut through the fence -- and at one spot Cousin Yura got his shirt torn on a jagged piece of the fence. Now we're getting the bags all rounded up, and before we can go, the official has more papers for us to sign! My mother tried to explain to them that they already had been approved in Moscow! But, never mind -- every official has to make his job seem like the most important position in the world -- including Moscow headquarters. The guy can't read English -- I can't read Russian -- and he's asking me what the English writing says on the paper! I explained it to him, and told him it's the same thing we had filled out before in Moscow -- he says, "Never mind! -- Fill it out again!" After a couple of times of rebutting the insanity of form-filing duplicity, "I," am now getting frustrated! Now the official is beginning to get irked and more bellicose, and HERE COMES, YURA! Now he starts giving the official some lip -- the official gets hot, and tells him how he looks like a bum, walking around with a torn shirt! That he ought to go home and have it sewn. Yura gets hot, now, and tells him if they had gates to walk through instead of torn fences he wouldn't have had a torn shirt! The official, keeps telling-me: Never mind, fill it out! Yura tells him, the redundancy is stupid! -- The guy gets madder. -- My mother gets upset worrying about us arguing, urging with me to fill the papers out and stop arguing -- and so help me -- because of his belligerency, if my mother hadn't been there -- Yura and I undoubtedly would have had a free trip to see our cousin in Siberia! (Even an

"Ambassador," like me, can get angry at times! But really, it wasn't personal; --- The issue with me was that, I was rebelling against the Totalitarian State, in defense of the oppressed! Nobody should have to live like a slave! --Blame Patrick Henry's influence! I should have sung "God Bless America" -- In His Face!)

We went to the "Authority" in the hotel, later, about getting permission to go to Verastan (Georgia)-- and they said, "Yes"! With the stipulation that, we would have to stay at a hotel, there. And the other option we had was to go to Kirovagan in about four days, for Uncle Marklen's sake, but mom was in no mood for travelling by car -- (she wasn't feeling too good) and we didn't go. We went back to Yura's, they had dinner ready, and after taking more pictures, we ate and drank again. Uncle Marklen, Yura and I brought mom back to the hotel so she could go to sleep early -- the strain of everything was getting to be too much for her.
The three of us walked around town, talking and looking at stores. I don't remember what triggered the mention of "Masiss" (Mt Ararat - pronounced: Ma-seess) and I remarked how much I had enjoyed reading Hovaness Shiraz's poem about it, and from "that," Yura said he knew where Shiraz lived and asked if I would like to meet him! "Like" to meet him?! -- Me?' -- A Self-Proclaimed poet! -- Hell, I'd "love" to meet him! (This was something I wrote a condensed story about, for The Armenia Weekly! -- It's a separate section at the end of this book.) After Shiraz's visit, we ended up at the hotel, in my room, and talked until 2:00 A.M.

September 17th:
Woke up at 7:30 A.M., called my mother at 8:20 - and we had breakfast in the hotel dining room. We went down to the lobby -- and sure-enough, waiting for us were, more relatives: -- Yura's brother Jora-and-his-son "Aramo," Tamara and her sister's daughter, and the neighbor who had brought them in his car. We go to Yura's at 10:00. I went with Yura to the lumberyard, again, where he works, and met one of my maternal-cousins. We spoke

with one of the men there and it seems everyone has the same disbelief, that life in the "States" is not as good as they've heard! -- Especially the wages!-- Well, it didn't take long to clarify "that!" -- Then Yura "told" me to tell the plant manager about my youngest daughter (16), Loretta -- how she had her own car (even though it was old) -- and you should have seen the look on this poor guys face! (I wasn't bragging about it; believe me -- just stating the fact. -- There's nothing unusual about teenagers owning a junky car in the USA!) The poor guy looked like he was going to cry. -- You could see his eyes getting watery, as he just stood there, somberly shaking his head in disbelief, mumbling unmentionables about his domineered lifestyle!

There was a junked car in the yard, and Yura said: "I'd even be happy if I could have that fixed up! ----"I could go on the rest of my life, dreaming, and I know I'll never have a car in this country!" That remark took me back almost 30 years, when I used to drive my own car to High School. It really saddened me to hear-him say that. And after what I've experienced there, I believed it! After you see people who even belong to the "Party," who haven't had cars in all their years, and still didn't, you come to the realization that it is a very stifling way of life! It's just another way of controlling the masses -- by bribery. (Be-a good boy, and maybe in 20 years you'll have an automobile. Behave yourself and your kids will go to college. -- Squeal (tell) on your neighbor and you'll get an apartment, sooner.) -- And then, conversely, we have our own problems in the "States," too, if you want to be objective about it" -- Send your boy to college (if you can afford it) and he won't have to go to Vietnam'! (How can one person's life be more precious and exempt from the Army-draft if he can go to college? Don't "poor" mothers love her sons?) Sell your soul to get somebody elected and he'll fix you up with an administrative job! Kiss the boss's rear-end and he'll fix you up with a good job! Pay some cops off and you won't get a ticket! ---- So, what the hell --- isn't the whole world corrupt?! Only the poor ol' souls in the world don't see life that way! They just see the negative things in life, because they're having a bad time. They don't see the life that some people consider the "positives," like the leaches of society who don't work because they're living off of the sweat of the working man's taxes, because of older excessively liberal laws. -- And "murder" on the streets, and you may not even go to jail, because some people can get the best lawyers. And people having to lock themselves up in their own homes, like prisoners, afraid to walk the streets at night because they may be robbed, or killed! -- Freedom? - We've got too much of it -- we abuse it! And "that's" the only thing they don't have in the Soviet Union! -- They can't believe an "American" can get into his car and drive across the Country without first getting permission from the Police Station! And that's, just to get approval to drive outside the city! --- Hell, this country would be full of Hinkleys, shooting Presidents -- (such as a nice man like Ronald Reagan,) if we had that problem! Both Superpowers dupe their masses into thinking "the other country" is our enemy, and wasting billions of workingman's dollars/rubles to keep those who are in power, in power --- or those who make millions, to make billions! It's good for Big Business. Maybe I'm getting old. I didn't use to think this way when I was young. The Russians wouldn't want to take over this country, the U.S.A.! Because they know that we would drive them crazy the first day! -- We're too liberated! Maybe everyone isn't as patriotic as me, in this country, but they would sure as hell rather be dead than be denied their freedom -- even though they wouldn't give their lives for their country! *(Hypocrisy "is" disconcerting!)

    Back to the story:

We came back to Yura's house --- (Note to reader: I'm having a guilt complex, not saying Aunt Ovsarina's house -- and I don't want to make it seem as if I've forgotten about her so soon -- but I can't use her name in the present tense anymore, so please forgive me! It shall always be Aunt Ovsanna's house, to me!) --- and Armen-Doda's daughter's-in-law ("harrss-err-uh") were there with their children. Cousin Leanna was there with Marietta. Shura and Leanna got into a family debate about her and her husband not getting along, and it became quite a heated discussion.

Yura and I went to the Shuga (market) so I could experience more of the Armenian daily life, and I took more pictures. We came back home in a round about way. --This was a part of town I hadn't seen before! If I had been caught taking pictures here, I'm sure I would have been reprimanded! There were large piles of dirt alongside the streets. And people were coming out of the holes that they had dug inside of them. -- And all they had were sheets of corrugated-steel covering the entrance-"doorways." ---- Don't ask me why, but the words from the Bible, in "Revelations" came to my mind- -- "Woe, woe, woe"-- as if the destruction of the world had already taken place'! ---- Here it was --30 years after World War 2 ---- and people (Armenians) were living like "this!" Right on the perimeter of town!

If Jesus would have appeared at that moment and asked me to give up my worldly possessions and follow Him -- I would have been "gone!" (My heart was being torn to pieces, witnessing the depths of deprivation! I could never have imagined people ever living like this! Someone once said that everything in life is relevant! And with that in mind, I guess now, you could say that the people living in the inner-city were living a "good" life, compared to these poor creatures that were living in the ground! But if I ever start thinking like "that" --- where I can philosophize anything into a non-entity --- I'll pray for The Good Lord to "strike me dead!" --- And to think how we complain about life in the U.S.A!)

September 18th:

As I was finishing my shower this morning, at 8:00 O'Clock, Yura had brought my cousins with him, Shura and Serrojh, from Shoulaver and Alaverdi. We spoke for a while, and later went to get my mother. Later, at Yura's, after a few drinks (as usual) and lunch, my mother and I were taken to go look for my paternal-cousin Davit's apartment ("Apartment" -- you know what that means?) It was a new section of Yerevan -- at a higher level in town. About 3-1/2 hours later, we found it! --We asked at his apartment complex (at his registry office) where he lives, and they looked for half-an-hour, and 10 books later, they found it! Aside from not having an index filing system, we found out later that they had changed apartment numbers, and they had "4 apartments" numbered, #9 !

    I met Davit and his wife "Svetta" and their 3 young girls -- and they came out to meet my mother. Later that night, at Yura's, after dinner and a few more drinks, Davit called, and they invited him over. We drank for a couple more hours, and unfortunately Davit couldn't drink, because he was driving. ----You could practically end up in Siberia if they catch you driving under the influence of alcohol!' Later, Davit drove us back to the hotel in his "Veeleess" (Willy's) jeep that he had borrowed from his friend.

September 19th:
I met the whole gang of tourists that I had come here with, this morning. And one woman was complaining how much she disliked it here. But, she had such a negative attitude about everything that I wondered why she even came on the trip! She had no relatives there, which, didn't help the situation, but if you can't be pleasant and communicate with people you won't be happy no matter where you go! People have a reason for being suspicious of strangers in foreign countries, don't forget, so you have to be more open and introduce yourself, before asking questions of strangers on the street. --- They will be more than happy to talk to you-- but you have to initiate it. Don't forget: you're not in the "States" where people are not reluctant to talk. ---- And here is an example: Two men contacted me as I stood outside the hotel. At first, I thought they may have been Secret Police, the way they looked around suspiciously, before talking. It was just like in the movies, so dramatic, they gave me the impression "I" was being watched! Even "I" started looking around' It was really funny! --- What the hell did I have to worry about?
I didn't do anything! -- Finally -- after we stopped turning our heads around, one of them started telling me that he had a

relative in Detroit -- and asked if I would contact them, when I returned home. The other man had a letter he wanted me to mail for him, when I "returned", because he felt they wouldn't let the letter go through. (Anything, for an Armenian.) - The one I tried to find was in California -- so I tried to relay the message through "The Organization," --(you know -- the one that is referred to as the "cloak and dagger" group! --It makes me laugh!--That shows you how little some people know about the A.R.F.) And the one that lived in Detroit, that was something else! When I called them and asked their last name just to make sure I had the right person --- there was a deathly silence! ---And even after I told them my name and where I lived, and why I was calling, they still didn't seem too eager to talk. I told them that I would mail them the letter and if they wanted to talk to me any further about the matter that I would be in Church, at St. Sarkis, in Dearborn, on Sunday. You would think someone would be happy to hear from an individual who's trying to contact-them from the old country. -- But, then again, who knows?

(Some of the men had to leave Armenia behind after the war. They had families there. And when they came to "America," they remarried, feeling they would never be able to see anyone from the old country again, because of the "Communists!" They may have been German prisoners of war, and after the war, they didn't want to live under Communism - and didn't want to go back to Armenia and live under Communist oppression, so they came to the "States." Or, who knows? They may have deserted the Russian army by deliberately becoming German prisoners of war and couldn't possibly go back to Armenia, since the Communists were still in power after the war! Don't forget! This was not the United States, where a man would give his life for his Country -- because he was protecting his freedom! The average Armenian didn't have that kind of freedom under Communism. Not the "freedom" as we Americans know it!

My mother had met an "old lady" earlier, and the woman, with her grandchildren, asked my mother if she would accompany her into the "American dollar store." My mother didn't know how the woman had come into possession of American money. (Someone from the States may have sent it to her with one of the tourists.) But she went with her so that the operators of the store wouldn't question the old lady of where she got the money, thinking she was a relative of my mother's. The store was across the street from the Ani Hotel. I said "old lady" because that's what my mother thought! My mother said she was embarrassed, and laughing at herself later, when she told me about it later! It was because the poor old lady looked so much older- than my mother, that she thought she was 80, and kept calling her "Myrreeg" (mother) until she found out that the woman was 10 years younger than my mother -- and my mother was 70. (Now you may understand why American women don't want to live in Armenia!) --- MY poor Aunt Ovsanna was the same way. She looked 10 years older than she was -- she had to work so hard -- and she was only 56 -- God rest her sweet soul -- my mother's youngest sister! -----------

Later, Yura and I went to his place of employment, where he finally got his vacation pay. They make about 1/4 of an American worker's pay, and their cost of living is about as much as ours. My three cousins and I went for a ride in one of my cousin's car, and we stopped at a roadside Inn and my cousins ordered some "Beeva" (Beer) and dried fish and bread. Serrojh took out the lungs of the fish and lit a match under it and it ballooned up until it burst. You should have seen the guys scrambling for it, like it was some kind of delicacy! -- Maybe it was some kind of game from their youth, who knows? -- But they were having fun! It's a good thing God created laughter -- for it helps to forget your sorrows. But, it only proves that life goes on -- and we can't stop it.

By the time we got back to Yura's, we ate again -- and the old-country boys had the liquor going again, making toasts to our dearly departed "Ovsan." Shura and Serojh were- really trying to outdo each other-, and before they were finished they were really feeling-good. Then, Shura said something that triggered off an argument, and he cried, apologetically, that he meant no harm. To cool things off, I suggested we go for a walk, down the hill by a little pond, a couple of blocks away. After another hour of talking, Yura had Shura crying again, as Yura wouldn't compromise. 'They finally stopped, and we got up and walked to a small restaurant near there, and they had another drink! (Don't these guys ever- stop?!) I drank lemonada. We ate some "khengallee" (whatever that was) and it was good. Later, as we were walking back to Yura's they asked me if I liked what we ate, and asked me if I remembered the name of it. I said: "Sure!" (and, jokingly said:) "Heen -Khallee" (which, in Armenian, means: "old rug.") And they burst out laughing. By this time, Shura was really "shot" -- inebriated -- but now, Yura wanted to drink to please, or placate Shura's heart! I guess he felt sorry for hurting his feelings. My mother and I were taken to the hotel by Jora and his wife, Maretta. -- And we sat and talked in my mother's room for about an hour. -- I went to bed at 12:30 A.M.

September 20th:
I woke up this morning at 6:30 and tried catching up with my notes. These memorable moments in my life that I feel necessary to record -- for God only knows when we may meet again -- or, if ever. Cousin Davit is taking me to Sardarapat this morning at 8:00 AM. He got here at 9:30, with a chauffeur-driven car. On the way to Sardarapat, there was a large hill named Moussa-Sar (or, -Lerr = mountain.) I don't know if it was named, or-inhabited by some of the villagers who may have escaped from the Genocide, or emigrated from "Moussa Dagh.") We were practically the only ones there, when we arrived. Maybe it was too early? I had previously heard the bells used to be rung at noon every day (as defiance to the Turks that the Armenians are still living!) They had built a memorial structured wall, with inscriptions proclaiming: "To the Heroes of the Battlefront" -- which was the last stand that the

Armenians (women and children included) made against the Turkish hordes, and it repelled the Turks, just before the First World War in 1918 -- which was when the Armenians joined the U.S. and the French in their battle against the Germans and the Turks-(whom the Germans had trained and supplied! Davit said that the bells are only rung on special occasions, now. (It just shows how much influence the Turks have on the Russians!)

If you are an Armenian, you can't help but feel a heart rending tug grip you. I know it may seem stupid, but something in me wanted me to cry out: "Hey, you Turks -- 'Sooren' is here!" The feeling of angered bitterness, knowing half of the Armenian population is living outside of its ancestral lands, because of the Turkish perpetrated Genocide of the Armenians! The Turkish beastly urge that lusted for blood-which only animals resort to when hungry. But these beasts were worse than animals. They were a disgrace to the animal world! -- They were Enver and Talaat Pasha -- whom the Turks revered as Gods!

They had a beautiful restaurant there, with mosaic murals on the walls. I took some pictures to show my brothers and sisters, who have become assimilated into the "American melting pot." On the way back we stopped at a newly constructed building that they called "Medzamor." Through the course of construction, they discovered ancient Armenian artifacts in the area, which proved that Armenians had grinding wheels, and one of the earliest furnaces known to man -- that meant, Armenians knew how to melt iron at that time. This proved that it existed prior to the Urartu era. They had an iron urn which, was used for collecting donations. They had a 2-foot clay (or cement) furnace with a spigot at the bottom, and it was used to melt ores, or metals, which used wood, and phosphors to intensify the heat. They even had a drinking vessel that had 6 vase-like tubes protruding from it, which showed that the Armenians knew about the planets at that time -- but only six of them. The polishing-wheel had bits of gold embedded in it, along with pieces of rice, which showed that they used rice as a polishing agent.

The young man was a college graduate, who was explaining things, but unfortunately I didn't grasp everything he was telling me because of my lack of Armenian education -- and I didn't have time to stay to have him explain everything to me at my level of comprehension. But I was allowed to take pictures of things, including the map, which showed the layout of the area at the time. I must reiterate, whatever they displayed, no matter where you visited, they had guides to explain everything very proficiently. Everything was first class. That's why they insisted you must go on guided tours on your first trip, so that you don't come back to your own country and complain that you didn't see everything. Or you didn't acquire satisfactory information --- which was the case on a couple of trips with my relatives who were not as informative -- but that's to be expected. Take my word for it, 'everything' is first class!

If you want to get out into the country and get some good Country music, and mingle with the village folks, go to the place called "Aghpyoora-ged" (spring-water-ground). We stopped there on our way back to town, to have a little snack. It was a radical transition from the suppressive lifestyle the people have to endure in town. They were really enjoying themselves.

Back in Yerevan, we stopped at an enormous restaurant, built near an small artificial lake, called "Sevan," probably to capitalize on the "Sevan" name - or maybe to placate those less fortunate Armenians who dream of going on vacation, or out of town. There were only about three tables filled! -I wondered why they built such a huge structure to have it sit so under-utilized, but I guess they must feel more superior, building (unnecessarily) large structures in the Soviet Union! --. Well, I guess that's one way of claiming they have no one on welfare! We ended up at Yura's, and ate and drank some more. Later, Davit and Svetta came over and we chatted until 11:OO P.M., and Davit drove us to the Hotel.

September 21st 1975:
After mother and I had breakfast this morning, we walked around outside until 10 O'clock and Yura and his wife Venerra came over and took us to their house. Yura and I took a walk around town, later. He wanted to buy some tickets at their famous theater, to take me to the stage play on my birthday. As we walked through some more stores in town, I couldn't help but notice the obvious attitudes of the store clerks and salespeople acting more Superior and dictatorial over the customers! My God -- these were all Armenians here -- but I guess they let -their jobs, or Soviet positions go to their heads! Even the President of the United States wouldn't talk to the average person on the street, like "that!") The salespeople were critical with the customers about not-touching the merchandise! (They sure have a lot to learn about salesmanship!) When some of the French dresses were put on display, they were instantly grabbed up, for I imagine they were more stylish than the Soviet product. -- It was not that the local product wasn't any good -- it was because they were too unfeminine and drab. The women knew what wanted! From the looks of it, the frills were in short supply. --- I couldn't blame them -- all women want to look feminine!

Momentary diversion again -- and prognostication. Remember, it's 1975:

I'm of the opinion that the Proletariat is paranoid about losing control of the masses, and must feel if they give the people everything they wanted that they eventually would start demanding a greater variety -- and if they couldn't meet their demands that the masses would get out of control! People will have more respect and patriotism for a government that allows them a freedom of choice. I personally do not expect Communism to exist by the 21 Century! In a world that is shrinking so fast, it is impossible to keep the masses ignorant, as they used to do in the dark ages! --The Soviets won't have to worry about belligerent adversaries, they're sitting on a ticking time-bomb of a speedily approaching revolution! -- Forty years have gone by since the world--war was over, and human nature dictates a yearning for peace and quiet. -- You may get by with the next generation's subservience, but when the generation after- that comes along - who haven't known about wars, you can't preach patriotism to them if there isn't anything there to offer a good life -- and they're going to rebel! They don't owe their country anything -- for their Country hasn't given them anything but suppression! The dictations of Karl Marx has, come full circle of what he was inciting "revolution" about! The masses are not sharing the fruits of their labor. -- There is no more "Queen Katerina" and "Nikolai Tsar" to think of their people as, "family.")

We came back to Yura's place, and mom and Yura played a game of "Tavli," or "Narrdi" as they call it (backgammon.) Later, Yura and I played three games of chess. I told him I'd drive him crazy -- but it was just the other way around. He ran circles around me!! He's too good! -- And I've been playing the game since I was in 7th grade at Salina School, in Dearborn -- right in front of the Ford Motor Company.

We conversed with the women and girls for a couple of hours, and shelled walnuts for the "choochkhall" they were going to make for us to bring home for the rest of the family. "Choochkhall" --- ah, you "foreigners" -- no offense, mind you --- it's just that when your an Armenian, or in that frame of mind, everybody else is a foreigner. -- You think the same way, don't you? -- As I was saying, about that funny sounding word, "Chooch-khall". It's an Armenian, sweet candy-like delicacy, made by threading a string through shelled walnuts, a few inches long. This is then dipped up-and-down into a pot of your favorite, hot jellied-fruit (i.e. apricot is a fruit frequently utilized in Armenia) similar to the process of making candles, until it looks like a long, fruit sausage! And when you're finished, you hang it up on a line to dry until it solidifies and becomes rubbery in texture. You can make it from apricots, prunes, apples, peaches, pears, etc. And you can preserve it for months! I'm convinced that this delicious treat has been made for many, many centuries, indeed. That was man's ingenuity for survival, something before refrigerators and freezers. -- As Socrates said: "'Necessity' is the mother of invention." And I confidently imagine "choochkhall" even preceded Socrates! -- Long before Armenians knew how to write; and passed it on from generation, to -generation! --- I love it! It takes me back to my childhood days when our mother used to make it. -- And those were "ice-box" days!'

But I was humored to think about the amount of dust and auto-fumes it was absorbing from the traffic going by, as it hung on the clothesline to dry, out in front of the house! But, what the hell -- if the Ford factory smoke we had to breathe in Dearborn didn't kill us, who's going to worry about ingesting a little more carcinogens and dust? Yura and his wife took us back to the hotel, and we talked for about an hour about life in "America" and our families.

September 22:
This morning my mother and I came down to the restaurant for breakfast, and waited for 20 minutes before we got served a cup of tea. I didn't want to be critical, to think they give you the royal treatment for the first three days, and then neglect you, after that. But after what I experienced, I don't believe it was just from a "shortage" of waiters, per se, because it seems the waiters give you the perfunctory service during the day, but at night -- when the nightclub and dancing business is going on-- they are really hopping! -- Because now, they are making big tips on their extracurricular activities. This is "Capitalism" now! (But be quiet don't tell anybody!) So now you know why the waiters aren't too energetic in the mornings, sometime. (Ah well -- don't say anything. Let them make a little extra money -- they need it more than we do. - They're our " yeghpyrrs" (brothers).
They had one waiter taking care of 30 people! Well, at least we had delicious "herreesa!" And "that" made up for all the inconvenience as far as I was concerned! Cousin Jora came walking through the restaurant, and I had to go running after him because he didn't see me waving at him. This enlightened me to

the other side of the restaurant, which was filled with French-Armenians, and they were really raising their voices! -- They made us look like pussy-cats. I guess they feel they're more sophisticated and that they don't have to tolerate that type of negligence. (I'm sure they're more sophisticated about restaurants -- since "food" is more of an "art" to them!)   Ah, 'cést la vie'! -- Whatever that means! That's French- Armenians for you. Aunts, Mariam and Armenouhi came walking over to our table. After they took my mother to Yura's house, and later, Jora and I went walking around town for about three hours. We got back in time for supper, and cousin Davit came to see me and was invited to join us. We took a ride around town in his borrowed Veeleess. About 9:30 P.M. He took us back to the Ani Hotel and we conversed for about an hour before he bid us goodnight. Then, a friend of my mother-in-law, Verkin Sargavakian Kevorkian came over and we conversed until 11:30. The man's name was Torkom Kevorkian -- a writer, at the Armenian Writer's Institute. My mother-in-law had previously written to him, informing him of our visit. He had fought alongside of Verkeen's brother, Apkar Sargavakian, and was a good friend of his. He said Apkar was shot and killed by the Turks, while riding his horse, approaching the battlefront with General Antranik. (Genocide era.) This man, "Torkom" must have been some man during his younger days. He looked like Victor Mc'Laughlin, or the John Wayne type; burly guy.

September 23rd -- My 49th birthday!
Woke up this morning at 7:30
Mom called and I went up to her room -- and Mrs. Helen Avedisian came from across the hall to join us for breakfast.
She said she was going to visit the other part of her family today. She said she was a little apprehensive about meeting the family that her husband had left behind --- due to circumstances of fate, and a matter of self-preservation from the yoke of the Russian Army! I imagine the Armenian men weren't the only ones to cross over into German territory, during, or immediately after the 2nd War, in order to escape the hell they anticipated encountering in

the repression of the post-war Soviet Union! There were soldiers from other Soviet Union nations that did the same thing! (I understand the Russians' KGB tried to track these "lost soldiers" down for years, following the war' -- Can you imagine their suspicions of 'being followed' - 30 years after the war?! - And in the United States, at that?! Well, after I've heard of the thousands of valiant Armenian men who courageously gave their lives to the Russian army because they were promised by Stalin that they would get their Armenian lands back from the Azerbaijanis, that Stalin had ceded to them -- I can't say that I blame them! -- For Stalin never kept his word!)

So, here was Helen, a little apprehensive, speaking in an excited and nervous, German-accented tone, about the unity, since she had never met any of them before. (Meeting total strangers whom you've heard so much about, and in an culture totally dissimilar/of what you're accustomed to, and in an, Armenian language that you are not capable of communicating in; I imagine you'd feel a little nervous, too!)
She told us later on, that, she was treated so wonderfully and warmly, that she was in tears, because she felt like a member of the family! (She just couldn't stop raving about it!) Well, that's, Armenians, for you! If they have practically nothing -- they still want to give you everything they have! We have a lot to learn from them, in the 'old Country.'

My mother and I, along with Yura, went to the American dollar store with the "old lady" my mother had promised yesterday, to go again, so she could buy the coat that she had looked at before. The woman wanted them to think it was my mother's money. The Russian bureaucracy wants to keep track of every dollar coming into the country! But, I guess that's another way of keeping the inflation down.   I

We got to Yura's house at 11:30 A.M. and my mother's father's-brother's son --"Ashot" came over as Yura and I were

playing "Narrdi.' (Now you may be wondering why I described "Ashot" that way, right? Well, when you know you're never going to have any relatives available, for you to meet in your life, you never take the interest to learn the difference -- to say -- my mother's maternal cousin. It was too overwhelming for me to try to remember all the names and relationships of those whom I was being introduced to -- which was a very small portion of them! -- I've even got a cousin in Siberia; whose father was my maternal uncle, who had married a German woman after the 2nd war and move to Siberia. -- Well, you can't stop love! -- And I imagine he may have felt he'd have less arguments about marrying someone -that was German, for obvious reasons. -- He died later, and my cousin is still there.)
I swear, my cousin Ashot looked just like Charlie Chaplin (in real life, not in the movies. -- And I doubt if -they've ever seen a Charlie Chaplin movie!) Cousin Seyran and his wife came in 5 minutes later -- we had lunch, and then Seyran took us to Etchmiadzin in a cab.

The town of Etchmiadzin, also the site of Armenia's Holy Cathedral; the Seat of the Patriarch -- built in the 7th Century AD. -- St Gregory, our Patron Saint, visited this site in Armenia, and became the Founder of Christianity. Armenians: first nation in the world to adopt Christianity as their State religion, in the year of 301 AD.

The Cathedral wasn't crowded, for it was a weekday. A young couple, 16 and 15 year olds, had come to church in their wedding attire, just to say a prayer. Our relatives wanted to purchase some small, gold necklace-crosses for gifts to the family, but they had difficulty finding a store or place where they could be purchased. (Obviously! USSR!) -- Well, if you can't find gold crosses in the Holy town, where else are you supposed to find them?

We went back to Yerevan, and after going to a few places, by word-of Mouth, we found a place that made them -- immediately upon ordering them! -- (Who knows -- they may have placed the molds a 1,000 feet underground, just to make sure they weren't found by the Russian dictators!)

We got back to Yura's for dinner -- and after we ate we had a few drinks/toasts with Uncle Ashot before he had to leave, for Tiflis, Georgia. Jora, Yura and their wives, and cousin Seyran's wife took me to the "Soondookian" Theatre for the stage play they wanted me to see on for my 49th birthday. The name of the play was "Harssanatsoo Hoossaseetch" (The Bride from the North.) There was an actor in the play who was the spitting image of my eldest brother Torkom (Ted!) What a haunting feeling that was -- to come to Armenia and see a guy on stage, who-looks like my brother!

The story was about a young Armenian man who was in love with a Russian girl (whom he taught how to speak Armenian) and their parents were going to meet each other, for the first time, to see if they were good-enough to marry each other! -- It was really funny -- but the most hilarious part was the way the Russian girl would roll her "R's" when she spoke Armenian -- which was over accentuated, to add to the hilarity! -- It was really, hilarious! -- But while everybody was laughing, including me, little did they realize that the tears coming from my eyes were from the emotional feelings I was encountering, just from hearing all the Armenian words in a stage play that made me yearn to be an Armenian citizen -- realizing that it could never become a reality, because I had my own family and country that I had to return to!! -- A country that offers me all the freedom that I want! -- A country that believes in God, and a freedom of religion! -- A country that offers you so much that, you can't help but feel patriotic toward. -- Rather than having the evil forces trying to force patriotism down your throat and make you feel that you're living in the best Union in the world -- while it's gradually slipping into decadence, because of it's emasculating dictatorship! -- (But if I was to brag like that to my relatives, they'd all Commit Suicide! -- And because I love them so much, I couldn't say anything like that!)

Yura and Venerra took us back to the hotel, and we talked for an hour before they bid us good night. (Hopefully someone in Armenia may have read some of Shakespeare's works -- where he said: "Stone walls do not a prison make, nor iron bars a cage." -- It may give them hope!)

September 24th:
I woke up this morning, and for some unknown reason the room was going 'round-and-round'! I swear -- I was holding onto the sides of the bed so hard, from fear that I was going to go flying off of the bed! -- That's how much the room was spinning around! I never had an experience like that in my life! You would think it would have happened on one of the other nights, when I had a lot to drink! I had to grope for things as I staggered to the bathroom! While I was being sick and throwing up, all I could see was green and yellow spit; nothing else. Disgusting. My mother was expecting me to call her for breakfast, and when I called, I told her I wasn't feeling too good. I didn't want to worry her. I really thought I was dying, I felt so bad (well, not really, but bad enough.) Before noon everyone was there; waiting and concerned about me.

(God must really love me, just knowing how-much people care for-me! And because I feel God loves me so much, that makes me cry! And sometimes I wonder why! -- Why me, God? - I'm nobody special in this world. -- And "that" is what keeps me trying to do things that are good in the sight of God - to please my Father! And He knows I'm far from being perfect! Yet, He knows I keep looking for things that He wants me to do! And if some people can't understand that, they shouldn't feel bad -- for, sometimes I don't understand it myself! -- But that's where my tranquility comes from!)

I couldn't go anywhere, so I told them I'd be fine -- so they left, leaving Yura behind for reassurance. -- My buddy! I finally got up, after about the fifth try, and we went to Yura's house. I finally threw up there, after a couple of hours.

Yura, Venerra, and Davit's Wife "Svetta" and I went to the opera. I couldn't very well say, "No." since they had already bought the tickets in advance. It was at the Spandarian Opera House. The seating arrangement was beautiful --- you didn't have to crane your neck around anybody to have a full view.

The opera was about the famed Armenian musician, "Sayat Nova." It lasted about three hours, and it was beautiful! The costumes were magnificent. -- Everything was first class! (It leaves you with the impression that if it's not first class, it's "off with their heads!" because everything seems to be flawless!)

I heard some of the tourists complaining about the stench in the restrooms. -- I guess the way some of the women were complaining it was even worse in the women's restroom! I changed my mind, as soon as I got to the bottom of the stairs -- the stench was so bad! I figured I'd go to the one I had seen underground, outside on the street. When I got to that one, I forgot about "going" altogether! It was so bad that the stench was discernable from the street!

It behooved me how they went to such great pains to impress people, and became totally negligent regarding the necessity of biological rudiments regarding toilets! Hopefully the "Soviets" may get the word via "Sooren."(Who knows, I may get to see my cousin in Siberia if they ever get their hands on me again!)

September 25th:
Davit called me this morning at 8:30, as I had just finished talking to my mother. He said he couldn't arrange things to be with me this evening, or to take me to the Armenian winery. He asked if it was possible to go tomorrow, and that he'd see me later.

The tourists were going to Dilijan, with their boxed-lunches today and weren't going to return until 9:OO P.M. ("Dilijan," I think every artist would consider it an artist's dream, regarding landscapes, -- It's really a picturesque part of the Armenian countryside!)

Mom and I during breakfast, conversed with some of the Armenians from Beirut. They said things weren't going too well in Lebanon, and mentioned how Beirut was once considered the "Paris" of Lebanon! The warring between the radical, rival factions had torn the city apart.

Cousin Yura met us at the door as we were coming out of the restaurant -- greeting us with his pleasant kind-of-usual smile. We kissed, and he hailed a cab, to take us to his house. Mom and Yura played "narrdi" (backgammon) and cousin Davit came over at noon. He had brought my paternal Uncle "Avo" with him, from Tiflis. I went out to greet him, and as I kissed him, he said in his soft voice:--"Ess onkom chee lahss." ("This time, don't cry"). He was referring to the first time I met him, 4 years ago and how our yearnings to meet had brought us to such emotional tears. I told him I wouldn't cry, but later, as I looked at him talking to my mother, I couldn't help keep the tears from welling up in my eyes. The thought of his resemblance to my father was too much. -- It brought back the yearnings for my dearly departed father, who had died in 1949, and it was like seeing again. That alone was worth the $1,500.00 expense of the trip! My brothers and sisters will never know how much they missed. They will never know the feelings of the attachment to their roots, to their ancestry, their relatives, their, father's country! I sometimes wonder where we got such dissimilar values! -- The 3 weeks there was like another lifetime. Some people go to Armenia too see the country. Here we have hundreds of relatives there, besides, and they still don't go! Doesn't ancestry mean anything to them?' Is it the materialistic, U.S. mentality that obfuscates their thoughts? But don't they have feelings?! --- My brothers and sisters? I cry just to think God made me that different! -- I must live a blessed life. -- "Park-Kez Asdvads!!" (Glory-to-You, God!)

Yura and I walked around town for a couple of hours looking for a "doodoog" (an Armenian, flutelike instrument.) The second place we went to had a better one, so we bought it for $14:00. The third place we went to, the guy wanted $25.00. -- The young man we bought the doodoog from said his father made it. I asked him his name and when he told me, I laughed. He laughed with me when I told him:"Wait until I get back to the United States and tell my friends I bought a 'doodoog' from 'Googeeg' in Armenia.

We were back at Yura's by 5:00 P.M., and about an hour- later-, we ate, again. -- Uncle Avo said he couldn't "Drink," that his stomach wasn't too good.

Poor Marretta, (Jora's wife) she's been cooking and cleaning every day like a slave, since we've been here, and she says: (with a smile) "What else is life all about for a wife, other than cooking and cleaning." And she's got three children - 6, 3, and 2 years old!

Davi't came by at 8:00 p.m. and about a half-hour later, took us to the hotel --- which is the first night mom and I have gotten any rest. -- And if we're tired, imagine how tired the working women are!

September 26th:

After having a good nights sleep, I wake up this morning still feeling a little light-headed. Mom called about 8:15 -- I had been up for an hour, lazing around. After breakfast, we stood out in front of the "Ani" and Yura came walking up with his usual, soft smile. We took a cab to his house. (When I say "cab" - it's usually a privately owned car, and the guys are making money hiring their services Out illegally, without a taxi-license -- and real taxi drivers' cars are usually black colored to be easily recognized by tourists; and they have licenses displayed in their cars.)

Yura and I had a chess game going, and about 10:00 Uncle Avo came over and we began conversing. I had heard my father tell me, when I was younger, that he was a "Bastheragaltsi"--and after talking with his brother "Avo," he told me it was really "Shirag", or Shiragal. (I guess 'the map shows Shiragi -- but names have been changed two or three times, in the past century, of some towns, because of the Turkish, or Russian dominance. In fact, I was told by some of my Russian-Armenian friends that the Russians deliberately changed names of towns, and distances, so the maps would be confusing to strangers, and for military reasons. I guess the "Ba" at the front of Shirag and the "tsi" at the end, is a connotation of a person who belongs to Shirag) -- just as the Greeks use the "apolis" on the end of some of their towns. "Ba"--- Shiragal -"tsi." -- he's a-Shiragal-resident.)

So, now I find out from my father's brother that Shirag, or Shiragal is about 12 kilometers (7 1/2 miles) West of the Leninakan border. And he says there are Russian and Turkish troops guarding the border -- and I couldn't cross over to the Turkish-held Armenian lands.

He told me that when World War 2 started, he joined the Russian army. Also, that his mother (my paternal grandmother) was starved to death by the Turkish Genocide of the Armenians, in 1918. He was wounded in the war, and had to use two crutches for some time. He said there are no more Armenians left there; and the soil is black there, (volcanic ash?) with gold in the soil. He said he had a son, in his 30's -- from his first wife -- and that he left her because of her infidelity. He has two other sons, Serojh 19, and another son 16, by his second wife.

Uncle Avo asked my mother if she played "narrdi" and she poked fun at him, telling him she could teach "him" how to play! (It was more in poking fun at each other -- her, in deriding him of his chauvinism -- and he, in ridiculing her of her liberated "American" ways.) -- So, as they played narrdi (and she beat him -- she's really good) Yura and I played chess. About half-an-hour later, some-more relatives came in from "Verastan" (Armenian name for "Georgia.") An hour-and-a-half later, they left, and then cousin Davit came over. Davit drove Yura and Venerra-and my mother and I to Venerra's father's residence for a previously planned, dinner invitation.

We drove about 11 miles into the country. Venerra's father had about an acre of land, privately owned, and he seemed to contain great pride in his accomplishment and possession, as he showed us his various vegetables and fruit trees. -- Everything that was growing there looked as if it was growing in very rich soil, for they looked so healthy and well sized. We met Venerra's two sisters, who were in their 30's. One of them had had a partial stroke and was left with a speech impediment. You could see the demeanor variance, from their "countryside" influence, in comparison to the women-folk raised in the city. They were so reserved and inhibited.

Davit and I had momentarily separated from the rest of them, and as we looked down the road a little ways, we saw a few young boys playing, comparable to what you would consider "marbles" -- but instead of using marbles, they were using "walnuts!" Also, instead of flicking them out of a closed fist, with your thumb, they were tossing them out, underhanded, trying to knock-out other walnuts that were there, in a four foot circle. Davit, youthfully spirited, ran over to the kids and talked him-self into playing, and hammed it up with the kids, who were near their teen years. He and the kids got a big laugh out of his gesticulations. The boys were bare-footed, and in "rags." How nostalgic -- It took me back to my youth, in the depression era. I wondered if that wasn't better than living in the U.S. cities and bumming around street corners, like our contemporary youth, bored to death, with nothing to do. --

- I wonder? -- No television sets around to make a robot out of you, Or to turn your thoughts toward violence from the fictional characters that influence your innocent mind, because of the realism of today's movies! ---Whatever happened to Charlie Chaplin movies? At least they evoked empathy, and you grew up caring for people!

The dinner was nice --especially when you consider Venerra's father did some of the cooking. -- His wife had passed away, years back. Yura's father-in-law and his son had a tiff with him prior to his marriage, because Yura wouldn't, or couldn't call his father-in-law "father." Yura said he had no recollection of his father (because he passed away so young -- so therefore couldn't know what a father was like.)

The conversation at the dinner table was polite and with amenities, but lacked gaiety, or a carefree feeling. We were there about three hours, and left after we ate because Davit had to go back to his job and check on the workers. Venerra's whole family struck me as being the serious type of people -- and they seemed to lack the spontaneity of cheerful disposition. --- But that's understandable, considering the life they lived/live under the Soviet regime -- and for that matter, the life all Armenians have lived -- so repressed and constantly-struggling with life's tribulations. I may have agreed with that way of life, because I feel God intended life to be a struggle, but, He also wants us to enjoy some happiness.

When we got back to Yura's, later, we talked for a few more hours, and then at 10:00 Davit and Svetta came over -- with Uncle Avo and we joked around and talked some more. My mother was ribbing Uncle Avo again, and it seemed Davit was getting a kick out of seeing our Uncle get harassed by my "American-liberated" mother. It was all in a humorous vein. We got back to the Ani Hotel at 11:30 and my Uncle Avo and Davit and Svetta came up for a few minutes, then bid us goodnight.

My dizziness has finally left me. -- How sweet it is!! Yet, a very-light chill came over me as I went to bed; and the temerature is 80 F.

September 27th:
Well, I woke up this morning feeling slightly dizzy. (I must have gotten food poisoning when all this started. I guess you can gradually build up an-immunity to all sorts of things as you get older. Heck, I figure if Socrates could build up an immunity to drinking poisonous hemlock, by drinking a little each day before they forced him to drink it-- and he survived -- I guess I'll live, too!)

After breakfast, my mother and I, along with cousin Jora and his wife Maretta went across the street to the American dollar store and waited for it to open. I saw Uncle Avo go into the hotel and I ran across the street and brought him to the store. I wanted to buy my Uncle an expensive suit, but he refused; and I practically had to beg him to at least let me buy him a less expensive one for 48 Rubles -- and then my mother got irritated about that! (Heck, I had enough trouble trying to get my "Soviet mentality" Uncle to accept it, and on the other hand I have to listen to my mother telling me about my "hard earned money'" -- Why do women have to put everything on a scale, in life?! -- Besides -- I only have one paternal and maternal Uncle, and if I can't honor them, what else is there to live for? I know my mother has read the Bible, but I don't think she ever read, or understood the part in the Book of John, where he said: "God loves a cheerful giver." -- God only knows how much longer my Uncle is going to live -- or me, for that matter! -- Or if I'll ever be able to see him again.) Mom bought Jora and his wife something, and then we all went to their house.

At noon, Uncle Avo, Yura and I went to the "guyarron" train station) and Uncle Avo bought his ticket for Tiflis, Georgia. I had Yura take our picture by the statue of our fabled hero (David of Sassoon) "Sassoontsi Davit" in front of the station. (I got the "word" that the Armenians had built the statue facing Turkey --

with Davit sitting on his horse, pointing his sword in "that" direction! The Turks must have complained to the Russians, and the Russians told the Armenians to turn the statue around! -- So the incorrigible Armenians turned the statue around but, they changed the position of Davits arm so that it was pointing backwards -- with the sword still pointing toward Turkey! -- "Ahbreek, yeghpayrnerrus!"

Yura and I walked through town, on the way back to his house, and we saw a man selling live fish. The man put about 3 or 4 fish on the scale and one fish jumped out and started jumping all over the sidewalk, giving us a laughed watching the vendor trying to catch it.

We went to the "sev-shuga" (privately operated marketers) and as we were walking around, I was taking pictures, again. And a man (official?) came around and started giving me some lip about taking pictures, and wanted to know if I was taking them to show the newspapers in the "States" -- also looking for things to criticize the USSR! As I began to explain, Yura interrupted, bellicosely, that it was just for my private use. (I thought we were going to go to Siberia, again!) -- but the guy just let pass off, with something like: "Alright --I heard you!" Boy -- as pleasant as my cousin Yura is in public, he sure isn't afraid to speak up to anyone!! -- I guess he doesn't believe in subjugation! (And I would probably have been like Yura also, if I lived there!) Some of the people have a country-peasant mentality, and would probably have bowed down to someone speaking to them in a threatening, authoritative voice. (I took some pictures of some of the vendors selling their goods there, and after I got back in the States and had them developed I mailed them to Yura to give to the vendors. I'm sure they would have gone a lifetime without a picture of their trade. It seemed to be a joke that people had to get a professional photographer to take their picture. What did the Russians think, the vendors' pictures might give away their military secrets?! -- To me, it was just another form of fear, or persecution!)

We got back to Yura's house and ate, then I played narrdi with my Uncle Avo. My cousin Reuben and his wife came over, and we took some more pictures. At 6:00 P.M. my Uncle Avo started getting nervous about missing his train--even though Yura kept insisting the train wasn't leaving until 7:30. So we walked him to the train station and got on the train with him, got him situated, and at 7:00, I hugged and kissed my Uncle goodbye, never knowing if I would ever see him again because of his age, and bid him farewell with a sad-hearted departure. -- My father's only, living brother!

I couldn't help but notice the passengers on the train, with their loaves of bread and sausages -- getting ready for the long journey. (You could say that I'm being facetious, for present-day Armenia is only, two-fifths the size of Michigan. -- But it sure takes you back, in time. It sort of reminded me of the "Dr.Zhivago" movie!)

We got back to Yura's house, and my father's sister was there, along with my 2nd-cousin Davit and his mother"-- who is her daughter. Davit's mother is my cousin, and is a doctor.)

I had never seen my paternal Aunt before -- nor had I ever communicated with her. (I guess my father never dreamt any of us would ever see them, and he never talked much about them, to us kids.)

My mother used to tell us stories about her childhood, so I knew more about her side of the family, brothers and sisters. -- In fact, my mother told us more about my father's-side of the family, than my father did! And unfortunately, our father passed away when I was 23, and at that age your brains aren't mature enough to start caring about ancestry. -- There was always an empty feeling within me. -- It seemed a part of me was missing! -- Especially when I used to see other kids with their relatives! --- God -- how I wanted and yearned for Aunts and Uncles and cousins! -- I felt like an immigrant, myself! -- In fact, I felt like I was "born" a foreigner! My two older brothers and I could only speak Armenian when we started Kindergarten, in Dearborn. --"Salina" School! Home of the foreigners, it seemed! -- (Those were the days when the Government didn't worry about air pollution from the Ford Motor Company; we inhaled it all! So, my father's sister and I hugged and kissed -- and with tears in our eyes, she kept saying, with an heart-aching voice: "Bahleeguss, yavroomeet merneem." ("My dear child, for your dear-ness(?), I'll die.") She kept kissing my hand and hugging me. (You could see the Turkish-language influence on Western Armenians --by the "yavroomeet" connotation. Armenians usually say "hokee-eet" -- "for your soul." (Years after our father died -- and I imagine my mother feeling she didn't have too many years left -- wanted to fill me in on my ancestry, told me that our father's mother had starved to death because of the Turkish perpetrated Genocide of the Armenians! Although my feelings of dearness could not have been any greater than they were for my Uncle Avo, I was spared the heart-rending emotions that I had had for my Uncle, because he looked just like my father -- and it was a heart-crushing experience! Davit had to leave -- and later, we had dinner and Reuben began making the oratorical, toasts.

After cousin Reuben left, Davit and Sveta came over about 8:30 and we talked and joked until 11:00 P.M. and Davit drove us to the Ani. We told him that we'd spend the day with them tomorrow. My mother and I have been coughing for the last 5 days -- (dry air, or dusty?)

September 28th:
Davit showed up at 10:30 this morning, and took us to the top of the City (Yerevan,) to his apartment-- It's called "Norkee Masseev." (The new portion, or area.) -- The city is growing so fast that they just can't build apartments fast enough! As apartments become available, they try to move the people into them and eliminate the old homes. Seeing this area is like a new, breath of life! Everything seems to be so spacious and clean. The

hills in the area are so gigantic -- like Pittsburgh, Pennsylvania, U.S.A.

Davit's three girls and his wife came down to meet us. We spent about three hours there, and Yura came over with the sister of my mother's lady-friend (Vera, in the U.S.) and her grandson -- who looked like singer "Tony Bennett" ("I left my heart in San Francisco.") Vera was an old friend of my mother -- they came to the U.S., together. Vera had been sending her sister money, for years -- trying to help her out. About an hour later, we had dinner -- and it looked like a feast for a King! Then, "Annigo" -- Davit's sister, played the piano for about an hour. It was concert music, and really enjoyable. She 'had been studying at the "Conservatory" --- and they "pay her" to learn! She said she had one more year before graduating.

We went back to Yura's, and about an hour later "Tony Bennett" suggested we go out to see some night, life. We ended up at the Ani Hotel's restaurant, where they were playing music -- more like a nightclub atmosphere. --- "Tony" really put on the spread -- you could see he was accustomed to this style of living! (You would think the guy was an American -- and in the "States," too boot! He had the waiter bring all types of meat and vegetables, and two bottles of cognac and some lemonada. ---- Then later, he had a tray of fruits brought over, and we sat around for 3 hours eating and drinking! They kept toasting everything under the Sun! We talked about life's contrasts, of both our countries, which was something to really see. I answered all the questions they asked as truthfully as possibly, without bragging, and it made me uncomfortable to see the dismayed and frustrated looks on their faces when they heard of the things they don't have, or even heard of. -- We were feeling pretty good by the time we left the place -- and I stopped drinking after I had 5 doubles! It must have cost about 24 bucks for the night, and "Tony Bennett" gave the waiter 28 bucks ($28.00) and told him to keep the change. You should have seen the look on the waiter's face; with a blush of pleasure! -- It probably takes him half a day to earn that much!

We went back to Yura's and picked mom and Vera's sister up by cab, and went back to the Ani about 12:30 A.M.

September 29th:
Woke up this morning not feeling dizzy -- (can't imagine why not, after last night!) As we were coming down to the restaurant, I was telling my mother about "Tony Bennett" and wondered what kind of position he's got. -- And my wise and knowledgeable mother told me about Vera sending her sister money -- (but the grandson "takes care of her!") -- ---- Yeah, I guess he takes care of her alright! The poor woman doesn't know what's happening to her money -- while "Tony" is living like there's no tomorrow!

All the Aunts, and Jora's wife, Maretta met us at the Ani and we took cabs to Yura's -- after waiting for Torkom Kevorkian, the writer, who didn't show up.

Uncle Marklen and Ovsanna's sons had gone to the cemetery to have a slab of concrete poured on top of Aunt Ovsan's grave. (The custom is, a year later, they place a large marble headstone on top of the slab.)

About 1:30 P.M. "Tony Bennett" and his grandmother showed up and we had lunch around 4:00. About 4:30 "Tony" and his grandmother left for Tiflis, Georgia. About 5:30 the men-folk came home and we all, drank until about 6:00 and cousin Reuben and his wife came over and we drank some more until, 7 P.M. Uncle Marklen only had about 3 drinks, and he was inebriated. He began talking -- slurring his words, and then he threw a shot-glass onto the floor and it shattered. -- Then he began explaining some kind of tradition of some sort to my mother (his oldest sister). -- And as I went to pick it up, hoping to make him regret doing it -- to also let him know that women are not men's slaves -- he held me back, and said "No.- don't touch it!" (The new bride, "Venerra" cleaned it up.) The women don't say very much when the men are drinking. -- Or even when they get drunk, for that matter! They just sit there and talk with each other.

About 15 minutes later, I motioned to Yura that we depart. We had planned on going to see Hovanness Shiraz, to pick up a book that he promised me; so we took a cab into town. We tried the apartment where we met him last -- and I think it was his wife who said he wasn't home. We left the cognac and candy that we had brought him and went to his writing apartment, where she said he, may be.

We walked across a Courtyard and up the steps to the second-floor. After knocking on his apartment door, we heard his voice, calling for us to come in. As we entered the dimly lit room, we reminded him of our previous acquaintance (since there were so many visitors coming to see him.) He stood up, as he acknowledged remembering us well, revealing the Outdoor shorts, he was doing his writing in, and warmly, welcomed us in. He turned the lights up, and you could see he was busy writing, with papers piled up on his desk. After he sat down, he took a book out of his desk, and asked me the names of my three girls and wrote them in the book -- regretfully chiding me for not giving them Armenian names. He seemed to be a man with very much dedication toward his country, and deep compassion toward his people. I thanked him for the book and a few minutes later, we were back in the streets. It was 8:30 P.M. and the town was bustling with denizens. We walked about 2 miles, back to Yura's. Uncle Marklen was put to bed by, mom's persuasion ----(he had gone out of his head and wanted to go back to Kirovagan) -- and mom said (in English): "You know, your Uncle is something else!"

Yura took us back to the hotel about 10:00 and we packed our suitcases -- and Yura bid us goodnight about 11:00. About a minute later, Davit and Svetta came in, and a few minutes later went up to my mother's room. I went to bed. -- It was going to be a long day, tomorrow. -- We would be leaving Yerevan!

September 30th:
The phone rang, and upon answering to my mother's voice, she asked: "Zartoon-ess, dugha, jon?" (Are you awake, boy, dear.) --- Here it is, 6:50 A.M. -- and I asked the management to "ring me" at 5:30 A.M. -- and they didn't call! -- About 7:05 Yura came walking in, and said Uncle Marklen was with him -- as he came straggling in, from behind. -- He looked very sober, but sad -- and Yura, later told me: "He didn't remember a thing he did last night!"

After breakfast, cheese, buttered toast, and "behrajhkee," this morning (like a hamburger-pie pizza, we went down to the lobby and everybody was there, except Jora's wife, Maretta and their kids. Aunt.Armenouhi told us her "pessa" (son-in-law) had gone berserk last night and chewed up the bed sheets! --(due to his alcoholism.) He drives a bus during the day -- and he seemed to be the quietest one in the bunch! (He looks like the typical Rebel, from Tennessee!)

We finally made it to the airport --- and the "cattle" stampede was on, again! --- It not only behooves me but, also dismays me to see how grown, "civilized" people can act like a bunch of cattle -- acting like they are not going to get a seat -- and worse yet, not even respecting the womenfolk, or their elders!

Mom didn't say anything to me -- and I thought everything was okay until we got to the passengers waiting room -- and then she said the crowd and the heat made her feel faint -- and that her heart was pounding! -- (Now, she tells me!)-- She took a glycerin pill, for her heart. I was quite concerned -- but she said she would be alright (probably not to worry me; for I know how she thinks!) In the other room, with Reuben, Marklen and Yura, I mentioned how mom was not feeling good, and that I was looking for a glass of water, and how that would help. -- Boy! -- You should have seen cousin, Reuben, jump! -- He really got shook up! (He's 61 years old --5ft.11 inches, and 235 pounds -- and he literally, was running! -- Maybe I shouldn't have said that. I was afraid "he" was going to have a heart attack!) ----- But, you know what?! -- Yura beat him to it! (The son-of-a-gun is really "jarrbeeg!" (smart and sharp). Mom drank the water and said she was feeling better. -- Yet, I had difficulty trying to slow her down; she still wanted to hurry to get a good seat on the plane! (That's all I would need, to have my mother die with a heart attack and my brothers and sisters back home would be blaming me! --- And she's acting like the ones I was criticizing!) Maybe we all become insecure when we get older? --- I had never seen my mother act that way before!

So here I am, writing with the roar of the airplane's propellers right alongside of me, on the wing! --- Had we been last, we would have been further back from the engines. It took 3-1/2 hours to arrive at the Moscow airport, and after a 15-minute "regrouping" we got on a bus and rode for another hour into town.

The Soviets had their bus drivers "conservation" trained, to take the 'bus out of gear and coast down the hills,' to save gasoline. I wondered, whether "we Americans" are too wasteful -- or was the gas shortage that critical?! I had been critical of the housing shortage in Moscow, when I was here just 4 years ago, because I had made a statement about the "shanty-towns" on the outskirts of town when we were landing here, in 1971. --- Well, let me tell you something'! As we were headed toward the city, while riding on the bus going 40 miles an hour, I saw apartment complexes, row after row, one behind the other, as far as I could see --- for over half-an-hour period! -- Some people may be critical of the "Soviet" system, as I myself am --- but You have to give credit where credit is due! --- They don't have the "boondoggling" bureaucracy as we have in Washington! -- I imagine when they want to eradicate their slums, they don't have to play politics, like we do! -- So -- as proud as I am of my Country (U.S.A.-- and I get goose-bumps when I sing the National Anthem) I feel there is a lot left to be desired -- especially the elimination of slums! -- But, "You," dear reader -- if you aren't pleased about "America" -- take a trip to most foreign countries and when you return, you'll be singing "God Bless America" or get a lump in your throat when you see the "Statue of Liberty! ---- God -- as much as we complain, we don't know how good we've got it, in the U.S.A.! --- And as much as we "complain" -- we should be thankful we have our "freedom of speech!" As Patrick, Henry, the American Revolutionary said, in 1775: "I know not what course others may take, but as for me; 'Give me liberty or give me death.'" -- "Revolutionary?!" --- Seems I've heard that word before!)

We arrived at the "Intourist Hotel" -- very modern. Mom and Helen got a room together -- and I got a room a couple of floors higher. (Maybe they recognized my rank as an A.R.F. member? Ha haaa.) Had a half-hour before lunch, so I cashed some travelers checks into rubles, in order to travel around, since foreign currency cannot be used in the Soviet Union, except at "American" dollar stores. We took a walk around town after dinner and got back in time for bed, at 11:OOP.M. --- Since, everything closes-up at 10:00 PM.

October 1st:
We had breakfast -At 8:30 this morning, and after, we took a bus tour around Moscow. The food and service was a radical transition, at lunch, and, in comparison, to Yerevan. --But of course, this was Moscow -- and they have to make sure they're-not outdone! It was first class service, and the food and tables were elegantly prepared. -- I never could understand why the restaurants were always situated on the 2nd floor, and you couldn't stop the elevator on the 2nd floor! At lunch, my mother and I were coming down the spiral staircase (figuring it would be easier for her heart, by walking down from the 3rd floor) and my mother missed her footing on the last step before the floor and fell down very hard on her knee and shoulder. --- I almost died, the way she fell. (I thought it was going to be much more critical than it was.) Why couldn't it have happened to me'! How stupid of me not to hold her arm until she got past the last step! I thought she

couldn't possibly get hurt -- she was looking right down at the steps, and I thought she knew there was one more step! -- Had she not been looking, I wouldn't have let go of her arm. She said later that she thought she was on the floor, and that's why I let go of her arm. Besides dying a thousand deaths, I felt very bad for the embarrassment that I caused her. -- I never before thought of my mother as "old" (in the sense that she wasn't capable of handling herself) but, I knew from then on that I would never "assume" again! (As light-hearted and spirited as she is, I have finally come to the realization that my mother has gotten old.) They didn't have a doctor in the hotel -- and the dummies didn't even know that there was a hospital one block away! My mother said the tour-guide girl took her in a cab, and they rode around town and then came back to the hotel area before they found the hospital! (Smart cab driver, I'd say -- that's one way of making a few extra rubles!)

In the evening, my mother's knee hurt too bad, and she didn't want to put pressure on it by walking, so she didn't go with me and Helen Avedisian, along with some of the others who went on a tour of the Subway system (which they called "Metro"). And this was a newer line. I completely changed my opinion about the Moscow subways not being as good as the one in Tiflisi! -- They had mosaic murals all over the walls and ceilings in their tunnels -- and even had huge chandeliers made of crystal, hanging from the ceilings! --- You could not possibly imagine anything that beautiful under the ground, after what you see what's above the ground. -- I mean it is exhilarating and breathtaking! I wouldn't want to try to imagine how long the decorations would last if it was in New York!

Life in Moscow is so drab -- You never see people smiling or laughing in the streets. They're so serious looking, or reflect the appearance that their conscious minds are on something else, like robots! -- Everything is so glum. The only exception to the previous remark, to really feel there is life in Moscow, is the movement of the people! They said that 5,000,000 people use the subways during the day! It's their major means of transportation. ---- And You have to see it to believe it. It's unbelievable. What a mass of humanity! The subway seemed to be about a 1000 feet under the ground's surface, according to my calibration. Later on, we went to "The" Circus! I emphasize "the" because it puts our state fair circus to shame. I had never seen a circus with "class" before. This circus in Moscow is for $3.00 -- and it includes checking your coat for no extra charge; and no-tipping, either! --- But more than that, when you're coming back out and want your coat, you just give them your stub and that coat is there in 2 seconds! The exterior of the building is all glass, and well lit. The trip to the circus, by subway, was only 10 minutes from the center of town. The lighting and seating arrangement was superb. No-heads to obscure your vision, because the seats were declined so that the row in front of you was low enough to see over the people's heads. -- And they had an "orchestra" -- not a band! The center ring area was built on a circular and hydraulically elevated platform, about 40 feet in diameter. And it lowers down to about 10 feet so the workers can place the necessary equipment onto the platform for the lion act. Just thinking that I didn't want to attend compels me to urge anyone reading this story to go without fail -- if you're ever in Moscow!! -- It's something to brag about; really!

The "Metro" system is a circular design with a network of 5 lines drawn across it; like cutting a pie. It's rare to find courteous people on the streets of Russia. Maybe it's because they subconsciously envy us "Americans," yet resent us for what we have. But then, I'm certain you'll find that in other countries where their citizens are deprived of the things they desire.

While we were touring inside of the Kremlin (wall) we were shown the world's largest cannon that was concocted by "Ivan The Great." -- It was never fired though, because the 30 inch cannonballs that were made for it, were never made to fit! (That's

what we were told. They probably didn't want to admit that they goofed. You'd probably blow the barrel apart trying to shoot a ball of that size! But the Russians have a mentality for enormity, anyway! The sight of it would have scared the enemy to death anyway, so, from a psychological standpoint, it may have served its purpose!
The guards were very cold-and-glaring as they watched us, and they seemed to feel their authority was beyond control! They had walkie-talkies pinned to their uniforms and controlled people from crossing the avenues of traffic that would allow the Proletariat officials to come zooming around the corners with undue caution, in their big, black limousines!

I tried taking a picture of the guard at the gate (from inside of the wall.) and another guard said: "Nyet" ("no") in a stern voice"'-. What a joke! What the hell is so special about a gate-guard at a Kremlin gate?! -- You would think I was trying to steal military secrets!! Sooooo, just to "cheesh" him off a little more, I deliberately held my camera in that direction, acting as if I was going to take a picture, and asked him if he said "nyet"?? and again he said "nyet" in an irritated voice. Being diplomatic is one thing, and following regulations is something else --- but this was absolutely, ridiculous! -- (Too bad my cousin Yura wasn't with me, we could have had a free plane ride to Siberia, to see our cousin.) -- Now if you think that's something, listen to this! -- They wouldn't let us take pictures inside of their main Cathedral (even without a flash!) Why did they even let us bring cameras inside the Kremlin walls if they are going to be so paranoid about it?! You'd think they deliberately said "no" just so they could jail some poor dummy who may think he could sneak a picture! --- Hey! Big brother had cameras watching you'all (as our Southern folks say down in Tennessee)!
The Cathedral had beautiful paintings of Christ and His disciples, and had the Tzars entombed in brass vaults "on" the Cathedral-floor, and about 54 more, of nobility, below the floor! The paintings were beautiful, and were from the 16th(?) century. I

asked the female guide if it was possible to purchase a book of the paintings that were on the walls. And she said: "NO, and, "If there were any, it would be hard to find." -- I guess if you want to see it, you'd have to go there to see it. In the 16th century, "Ivan The Terrible" asked the architect if he could build another Cathedral like the one he built - and after saying "yes"- Ivan had him blinded! ---- An Atheist government enshrining and protecting religious paintings and churches?! They said only the older folks go to church, now. It seems they try to keep everyone in ignorance of the majority of the transpiration in order to instill an inadequacy complex, so that the superior ones can maintain control!

We went to the Canadian Embassy, in town, and it was in the more-common residence. They were very cordial, with all smiles, and spoke to the group and answered questions of the (mostly) Canadian tourists (since we took the plane out of Toronto and Montreal.) I was left with the impression that the Canadian Consulate employees didn't seem to rate like the U.S. people; even though they had done more business transactions with the Russians.

October 2nd: 1975
The porter's knock on the door this morning was right on schedule; 6:30 A.M. I allowed him access to my luggage in order for him to load it on the bus. After a knockwurst-like sausage for breakfast, we got on the buses at 9:10 and went to the airport. After about 3 hours of customs inspection, we were on our way.
While we were at Customs, we thought we were really in for a hard time, because they started going through purses and suitcases with a fine-tooth comb! They scrutinized the "declarations" slips with an eagle eye to see if the money count and the gold rings tallied (to the declarations we filed when we entered the country!) Imagine having to declare my gold plated high-school ring on the declarations when I entered the Country? I tried to tell them it wasn't worth anything -- but the official, in a

demanding tone said: "Mark it down, anyway!"--- Imagine, that?!) But when "we" (from the USA) got there, they were casual about it and didn't even check half of our luggage. (This was their policy to hang you if they didn't like you, by scrutinizing all the money and gold that you brought into the country, And if there was any error, or if you may have publicly spoken condescendingly, about the Soviets, they could make it very difficult for you! You have to prove where your money went by showing them your sales slips! -- That's one way to keep inflation down, and also make sure no Soviet gets rich and rebuts regulations. Although the American dollar was supposed to be worth less than the Ruble, it was in actuality, worth 10 times more on the black market! Imagine someone gladly paying $90,000.00) for an automobile?! It was happening! I guess a few of the people from Canada were "Beirut" émigrés, and they were particularly selected, for it was suspected they have more dealings with gold, and surreptitious dealings.

We left Moscow at 1325 hours (I:25 P.M.) and landed in Paris at 1700 hours. Left Paris at 1825 hours and landed in Montreal at 240 hours, October 3rd.

From Montreal it took us 45 minutes to land in Toronto. -- Helen's husband was there to pick us up. It was nice to see the way her husband ran up to her to kiss her. --- You would think he wasn't expecting her to come back!

When we got to the Ambassador Bridge, in Windsor, to cross over into Detroit, I thought sure as hell we were going to get a grand inspection! -- Here's an Armenian, Helen's husband, with a Russian-Armenian accent, and Helen with a German accent, my mother with an Russia-Armenian accent! -- and I was "born" in Pennsylvania! And, it's about 3:00 A.M. (What better time to smuggle something, "right?!" -- The Customs' man asked us where we were born, where we were coming from, and said-."Okay, go ahead."---- (??!!!! --What ? No Inspection?!) Well --

that's twice I've come from Moscow -- and twice (New York last time) they didn't even check Our bags!! --- Now that ought to tell you something about the confidence they have in the Russian inspections! -- They know you've been checked, very closely!

****** Writer's Final Note: People die trying to get into this country (USA) ---- And you know what? After the countries I've been to, I would say it's worth taking that chance!

Sincerely: Sooren Simon Apkarian

P.S.: Hope you liked the story. Maybe my Grandchildren may read this some day and learn a little about Grandpa "Sooren."
There's over 100 hours involved in writing, editing and typing this once-in-a-lifetime story. Hopefully my relatives may get a copy of this to remember the only Durian/Apkarian they ever saw, from the "United States of America," was their loved one, named "Sooren."

"The Armenian Heritage" goes on. --- "Turks"-- you didn't succeed!
And some day, we'll get our lands back, because "Sooren" said so! For "Jesus" said: "The meek shall inherit the earth." Our Armenia!

***** But, "Readers, "-- please! When you speak about "Western Armenia" -- don't say "Turkish"-Armenia, say: "Turkish-Held Armenian-Territories!" (We want --T.H.A.T.)

I dedicate this book to the memory of my loving, immigrant Armenian parents; Simon and Varsenik (Dourian) Apkarian. -- Also, to all my loving relatives - living and dead -- who contributed to my thoughts, added to *my* ancestry, the wealth of my life -- The Armenian Heritage.

Typing Completed in the 70th yr. of the Armenian Genocide: April 24, 1985 and retyped into my Computer (with additional hours of the Armenian Genocide. 1995 in the 80th year.)

A Highly Personal Discourse and summation of my reflections of Armenia. September 23, 1973
No one but an ancestral Armenian on foreign soil can understand or appreciate what it's like to visit the "homeland" --- until they, themselves trod the soil of Armenia.

Naturally, we heard about "Haiasdan" (Armenia) from our- parents (or other Armenians,) but WE transmitted those tales to the remote or subconscious recesses of our minds, only to be dreamt of as a distant land of heritage which, we probably would never see! Unfortunately, because of this process of thought, we have created a negative conditioning to which we have subconsciously accepted, and have become victims. Those of you who share similar dreams, or have aspirations in assisting in regaining the "homeland," I say to you: "Don't wait, or don't dream; be more positive in your thoughts. You can and must go there as soon as possible, in order to generate the love for Armenia, which awaits you. Then, and only then will you be inspired to such an extent that upon your return to the "States" you will react with a burning passion to accomplish your goals, and will generate the enthusiasm of others around you. Those of you in the younger generation are more fortunate, because of the liberalization of the times. You are capable of traversing distances which, we wouldn't have dreamt of during our Youth. Don't allow you aspirations to become mired by the stagnation of age. Secondly; the younger generation has changed its outlook on the "materialism" obsession in America, and will not easily be indoctrinated by this system. Presumably, and with this thought in mind, they will have more time and financial means to channel toward their direction of appeal. (Hopefully: "Hai-Tahd").

I think most, of the "concerned" Armenians, subconsciously feel that if Armenia is eventually regained that, they will be too old, or too accustomed to their materialistic way of life. That they couldn't possibly consider returning (or going) to Armenia; and therefore, are not really involving themselves to their fullest extent!

I sometimes wonder just what we Armenians are trying to do. Do we really want to regain "Hyasdan" (Armenia)? If so, we seem to be going in the wrong direction. One would think that at the rate we're building schools and churches here in America that, we're trying to build a "Hyasdan" (Armenia) in the "States." Are we eventually going to end up with an Armenian society that's going to say: "Hyasdan (Armenia) ... who needs it?"
I'm all in favor of schools and churches but, I hope we don't lose sight of our goal with these lesser important aspects. If we are going to regain Armenia, now is the most opportune time. I believe the youth of the world presently is fighting a war against hypocrisy and dictatorship. The U.N. is still in the United States and at Our doorstep. (Who knows when they may decide to move to another country?) The public and the world is aware of our anti-Turkish sentiment; and Russia would like to take advantage of our (U.S. vs. Turkish) relationship. The African nations have a majority-Bloc-Vote in the U.N. and are against genocide, who (including Russia or U.S.) is going to jeopardize their relationship with them, when we presently have a world fuel crisis?
So, you tell me ... how can we proudly say: "Armenians were the first to accept Christianity" and not give Our lives to regain our land? The newly reconstructed "Erebuni" (where Armenians sacrificed their lives to God, rather than accept fire-worshiping) has risen from ruins to show us what courage we Christians had; and today, an anti-Christian country holds our land!! The greatest enemy an Armenian has is his own arrogance. He should learn to use it on Turks ... instead of other Armenians!

Torkom Kevorkian & Victoria Apkarian's Uncle, Apkar Sargavakian

Both men fought the Turks in General Antranik's Army, circa 1917. Verkeen said she had a brother named "**Apkar**" who came to the United States in 1914, and returned to **Armenia** in 1915 to join the army. He fought alongside General Antranik, against the Turks, and was shot and killed while riding his horse, advancing the enemy line at the Russian-Turkish border. (His death was verified by a man I met named **Torkom Kevorkian**, in 1975, when I went to Armenia for the second time. --- He said he fought alongside 'Apkar' and saw him fall off of his horse after being shot. They were good friends.) **Apkar was Verkeen Kevorkian's brother.**

Some ironies of contemplation: "**Torkom**" was my eldest brother's name. **Apkar**ian is my last name. **Kevorkian** was my wife's maiden name. **Antranik** is also, my brother-in-law's name.

```
                          Note by: Sooren Simon Apkarian
Page 97 B -- Excerpted from Sooren's book: The Armenian Heritage
```

www.ingramcontent.com/pod-product-compliance
Lightning Source LLC
Chambersburg PA
CBHW031359040426
42444CB00005B/349